And Now We Have Everything

And Now We Have Everything

On Motherhood Before I Was Ready

Meaghan O'Connell

Little, Brown and Company

New York   Boston   London

Little, Brown and Company
Hachette Book Group
1290 Avenue of the Americas, New York, NY 10104
littlebrown.com

First Edition: April 2018

Little, Brown and Company is a division of Hachette Book Group, Inc. The Little, Brown name and logo are trademarks of Hachette Book Group, Inc.

The publisher is not responsible for websites (or their content) that are not owned by the publisher.

The Hachette Speakers Bureau provides a wide range of authors for speaking events. To find out more, go to hachettespeakersbureau.com or call (866) 376-6591.

"A Birth Story" is an edited and expanded version of an essay published on *Longreads* in November 2014. "Slacker Parent" is an edited and expanded combination of two essays published on *New York* magazine's website *The Cut:* "Trying to Make Mom Friends Is the Worst" (December 2014) and "I Am the Slacker Parent" (February 2015).

ISBN 978-0-316-39384-3
LCCN 2017956688

10 9 8 7 6 5 4 3 2 1

LSC-C

Printed in the United States of America

Contents

For D.K.

Who has not asked himself at some time or other: am I a monster or is this what it means to be a person?

—Clarice Lispector, *The Hour of the Star*

Oh dear, they say. Poor baby. They do not mean me.

—Rachel Cusk, *A Life's Work*

And Now We Have Everything

Baby Fever

A BABY WAS the thing we were trying to keep out. A baby was a consequence. A fuckup. Or it had been until recently, when, like a joke that slowly becomes sincere, I started imagining myself pregnant in a nightgown. Strangely, I never imagined the baby. Only me, a mother. How it might change me or wake me up. Make me better.

I had a hunch I was pregnant when we rode our bikes to the book fair on a Sunday in mid-September. We were taking wide turns through backstreets—the air perfect, the sun just out—and suddenly I stopped in the middle of the road, unable to keep pedaling. "Hey!" I called after Dustin and he looked back from his bike and gestured over his shoulder for me to keep going. When I didn't he looped back to me and stopped, one foot on the ground, one still hooked into a pedal.

"We're almost there," he said, "come on," and rode off without asking me if I was okay. I was confused by my body, near tears, and now full of little-kid rages at this man I loved and his disregard. I got off my bike, shaking my head, and spite-walked beside it along the side of the road. I hated him. I'd just agreed to marry him the week before, which made every interaction between us extra-meaningful. I wasn't just calling after him on my bike today, I was facing a lifetime of it.

And now I had this hunch, a feeling—call it women's intuition—centered in my tits, which at first simply ached and now were full-on itching, like an allergic reaction to all of this. I was sure, scared of how sure I was.

He came back. "What's up?"

"I don't know," I lied, really crying then. "It's fine." There was so often no way to tell the truth without it sounding like a whine. I wanted to be strong, to shrug it off, shake it off, as ever, wait it out, give him the finger. But I knew. I had no proof, no test, just this body that I'd presided over for twenty-nine years, a mystery still. There was no note, no alarm sounded, just the quiet organization of cells while you wait to be let in on the joke.

"I *still* haven't gotten my period," I had said to Dustin that morning when we were getting dressed.

"You say this every month, though," he'd said. He wasn't wrong. I was one of those women who managed to be caught off guard every single month when their periods came. I never had a tampon on me when I needed one. I had the litany of pregnancy symptoms memorized, though. All women do.

"Okay, okay," I said, raising my hands in surrender. I didn't mention that the night before I had to look away from *The Sopranos* on my laptop during a bar scene at the Bada Bing. The strippers' breasts, full of silicone, looked like mine felt.

I figured either I was right and would be able to say *I told you so* or I was wrong and this would go down as just another week spent in suspense, obsessively Googling my symptoms with that jumpy, forbidden feeling, wondering what I'd do.

Just one more week spent thinking about what I'd read on the internet once: that leftover sperm can live in a man's urethra for a few hours, and if he jerks off right before he has sex with you? Even if he pulls out, you're doomed. Or blessed, depending on how you look at it, although who wanted a baby from that piss sperm anyway? It was quite a mental image, blown up in the microscope of my mind's eye, sperm like pinworms crawling around that mysterious hole at the tip.

When I was in the eighth grade, my teacher kept me after class because she'd found a torn-out article in my desk from *Cosmopolitan* magazine wherein the author assured an inquiring naïf that no, you couldn't get pregnant from making out in the hot tub. "I'm concerned," my teacher said. I had been too, until I read the article. My best friend had brought it to school for me after I'd spent her birthday party rubbing against my boyfriend's public erection in the swimming pool.

We were just that week deep into Googling wedding places. Or I was. We were talking about doing it in Montauk in early spring. On a sand dune or in a state park or somewhere cheap enough that we wouldn't have to go to our parents for money. When Dustin got down on one knee and asked me if I'd think about marrying him, we were on a mountain, had just stopped to pee in the woods. He said it like that— "Will you think about marrying me?"—and I laughed, because, well, hadn't I been thinking about it pretty much nonstop since I'd met him?

Before it was official we'd broached the subject over dinner every few months. The marriage question. There was no definitive position, or if there was, it was always shifting. Once I overheard him tell someone at a work party (mine) that he would be happy to stay with "someone" forever, have babies together, and never get married. He didn't see the point of a wedding. I suspected he just really hated to dance.

Some days I couldn't tell whether I wanted marriage or

not. Were the parts of me that resisted just trained to construct elaborate rationalizations for why I didn't want this thing I might not get anyway? And weren't the hesitations all some version of *It might not work out*? Sometimes it felt like I spent my whole life trying to tell the difference between fear and circumspection. I was always trying not to want things.

I knew I could convince Dustin to get married; he had told me as much: "You wanting it makes me want it too." But did I want it enough for both of us? Did I want to be married enough to campaign for it and risk taking the blame if things went south?

Then I would go for long runs around the neighborhood and cry, imagining us dancing on our wedding day to Sufjan songs or some shit.

On one particular night in a restaurant, he raised his glass, nodded in this sexy, decisive way, and said, "Let's do it, let's get married! When should we get married?" I shrugged and laughed in his face.

"I dunno," I said, as if all of me hadn't just risen up and sighed with relief.

"Come on," he said, exactly like I'd always wanted him to.

We walked home arm in arm that night, giddy, but then I lay in bed wondering, was that it? Were we engaged? Should I tell my friends? (Answers: No; no; no.)

I cried when he finally did propose to me on that

mountain, not because we loved each other and it was beautiful but because he looked so vulnerable, so silly down there on the ground, gazing up at me with little-boy eyes, doing it just for me. I felt like I saw the whole history of him, his boyhood, his teenage years, and I was in love with all of it. I said yes to all of him. He put a ring on my finger, one I'd pointedly sent him a link to on Gchat a few months earlier. (ME: I like this ring, ha. HIM: Oh, really?) It had a small turquoise stone next to a diamond, tiny and antique. I twisted it around my finger, privately and inevitably worrying marriage was a mistake as we hiked up and then down the stupid mountain in our sneakers and jean shorts.

By the time we got back to the car at the bottom, I was done freaking out. I looked at him in the driver's seat. *Oh. It's you,* I thought, and felt a wave of peace wash over me. How good it was to have something I was scared to want but wanted all the same. When we had sex that night—we had to; how could we not?—I told him it was fine, he didn't need to pull out, my period had just ended, don't worry about it.

Now we had been officially engaged for a week, and my woman's intuition and I were mentally canceling all of my wedding fantasies.

At home that night after the book fair, we unpacked all the books we'd gotten. I was getting ready to meet

my friends for a drink at a bar around the corner and
I stopped mid-shirt-change to scratch my boobs. Dustin
looked at me.

"How would your grandma feel about a shotgun wedding?" he said. We laughed but then got quiet, suddenly
needing things on opposite sides of the apartment. A bobby
pin, a pair of socks.

I walked to meet my friends at a restaurant a few blocks
from our apartment. I found Halle and Sara at the end
of the bar, talking about some night they'd spent there together recently. Lindsay was late but would inevitably show
up perfectly dressed and maybe with Brian, whom she was
going to marry in less than two months. We'd all been
friends for years by then, since our early twenties. Halle
and I had gone to school together at Notre Dame and both
ended up leaving our Midwestern Catholic university to
move to New York City—Halle to go to library school,
me to be a live-in nanny. She was funnier than me, wilder
and crasser and more outgoing. I was her straight man,
always shocking her with my naïveté. ("He said he really
liked me, but then after we had sex he never called!" "Oh,
Meaghan...") Ultimately both our short- and long-term
goals were the same: (1) lose our virginity; (2) find love;
(3) make enough money to stop shopping at Forever 21;
(4) become famous writers.

* * *

Halle had introduced me to Lindsay, a tall, beautiful art history major who moved to the city a year after we did and also had no idea what she wanted to do with her life aside from watch reality TV with us all weekend and complain about men. I met Sara when I interned for her at a kids' writing center in Park Slope. She was a year older and had gone to college in the city and so was light-years ahead of us in terms of worldliness, which is to say she knew what restaurants to go to in each neighborhood and had an established brand of cigarettes. We hung out and did what young people do: reenacted weird encounters, overanalyzed text messages, made grand plans to exercise and never followed through. We'd all grown up religious and had a shared guilt, a shared self-loathing, and a shared dark humor. We were miserable half the time but also sure things would work out eventually.

Now that we were approaching thirty we'd coached one another through countless disappointing nonrelationships and had slowly shuffled our way from shit jobs to work we actually wanted to be doing, or at least work we didn't have to feel bad about when some asshole at a party asked, "So, what do you do?" Somewhere around twenty-six or twenty-seven we had started taking better care of ourselves, drinking less, cooking more, getting our hair dyed at the salon instead of using a box at home. Maybe what I'm saying is we just had more money.

Lindsay and I had been more hapless, romantically, than the other two, but now we were both basically settled down, separately trying to figure out how to balance our deep friendships with the desire to cocoon up with these men in our increasingly cute apartments. But my sounding board was still these three women, the first people I thought to tell anything.

Lindsay got there, and as we sat down at the corner booth, I was impatient, waiting for everyone to order so I could make my announcement.

"So, guys," I said once we all had our drinks. They all looked at me expectantly. "I don't know really when my period was due but I think it's late. I think I'm pregnant." I had an imaginary flashlight under my chin. "*And* my boobs hurt!" I expected a chorus of gasps but they seemed unfazed. In fairness, this was how we'd spent most of the past decade: huddled in the corner of a bar convinced we were pregnant even when it wasn't possible. It was our form of disaster preparedness, our emotional earthquake kit. "I mean, yeah, he wore a condom but you never know—" Was there some excitement there underneath the performance of panic? "I'd have to get a new job. Or move home and live with my mom? Or move in with him in Queens, depending on how he reacted, of course." It was a way of checking in on your life, on what you'd be willing to lose if everything changed. Didn't everything changing hold some appeal?

"I could always get a job, right?" I said. "Get health insurance." Months earlier I had sat at the same corner booth at the same bar and announced I was leaving my cushy tech job, where I made seventy-five thousand dollars a year doing copywriting with a bunch of other young people.

"Well, did you take a test?" Halle asked now, a fair question.

"No," I said. "I will." I knew she understood why I hadn't done it yet. There was something appealing about the not-knowing, living in suspense, trading worst-case scenarios, watching our friends react, watching ourselves react. We treated the possibility of pregnancy as a sort of litmus test: Were we grown up enough to have a baby? Nine times out of ten our worrying was unwarranted, but on the rare morning-after that it was, we just went to the corner store and bought Plan B. ("What if it doesn't work?" I said to Sara on one such Plan B afternoon. Later she told me I had a twinkle in my eye when I said it, like I was hoping it wouldn't.)

"I'm sure you're not pregnant," Lindsay said. "I'm sure it's just stress."

"Yeah," I said, suddenly feeling stupid for bringing it up. I turned to Lindsay. "What about you, are you freaking out?"

Lindsay was about to have the kind of wedding you see in

magazines, with a big champagne-pink dress and invitations designed by her soon-to-be-husband, who was goofy and kind and whom Halle, Sara, and I loved almost as much as we loved her. I had sat on the stoop of Lindsay's apartment many times over the years trying to reassure her she wouldn't die alone. Sure, her wedding was real and my pregnancy was only hypothetical, but in my head I was still vowing to prove her wrong.

Back when Dustin and I first met, I told him over some postcoital breakfast (which they all were then) that I wanted to have a baby by the time I was thirty. I was twenty-six then; thirty still felt far enough away that I could say something like that.

He made an exaggerated gulp. "Well, okay," he said, laughing, putting bread in the toaster. He was twenty-eight and working in a bookstore in Lower Manhattan, where I'd met him. I'd known of him for a while; he was the cute guy who tweeted funny things on behalf of the bookstore, the guy who hated Jonathan Franzen, the guy who wore suspenders and blue jeans and rode his bike everywhere. I wasn't sure whether to swoon or roll my eyes. Both.

The afternoon I finally met him, my voice shook as I spoke and I felt faint, leaning on the New Fiction table. We spent weeks sending each other late-night e-mails until he broke up with his girlfriend. Before I met him, I'd spent a few years having sex with strangers and falling in love with guys who didn't love me back, small dramas my friends coached me through or distracted me from but that had left me feeling, if not hopeless, then jaded. Reckless. I told Dustin all about my latest heartbreak the first night we spent together and was shocked when I looked up and saw I'd made him cry. My first real boyfriend. I was madly in love with him, full of disbelief at how easy and obvious and scary it all felt. I didn't know what to do other than pace around my tiny apartment—the first and last apartment that I lived in alone—feeling like I was going to burst with . . . feeling.

"I love you," I whispered at him one night when I was sick and I thought he was asleep. He gasped, opened his eyes, and said, "I heard that." The next day he said he'd marry me if I wanted him to, that he'd never thought marriage or children were for him, but he'd do whatever I wanted. Thirty was so far away. It was just an idea. I was being stupid, of course. We shook our heads and buttered our toast.

"Promise me," I'd told Halle earlier that year, after I quit my job but before Dustin and I got engaged, "promise me you won't let me have a baby before I write a book." She agreed, nodding as we crossed the street on our way to a coffee shop.

"If you start talking about having a baby soon, I'll slap you," she said. "I promise."

"Good," I said. "Because I'm starting to see the appeal. You have sex and then it just happens to you. At you. You don't have to do it yourself, every day, out of nothing. And I'd have the perfect excuse to never write again."

"Exactly."

I'd been with Dustin for three years then and the subject of babies felt more dangerous than ever. When he and I walked around the city and passed storefronts with baby clothes in the window, I held my breath, averted my eyes. I told him, in what I hoped was a neutral tone of voice, about cousins or old roommates getting pregnant. Just stating the facts. I handed him my phone in the dark of our bedroom with a daring "Look at this baby!" As if maybe if one of them was cute enough he'd sit up in bed, look into my eyes, and say, *Let's do it. Let's have a child together.*

Avoiding the subject with him meant hiding on the other side of our railroad apartment and reading worst-case-scenario birth stories of strangers on the internet. I'd send the scarier ones to Halle. Subject: harrowing!

Oh my Godddddddd, she'd reply, then she'd send me a link to the personal blog of someone with eight kids or a debilitating disease.

Motherhood was the farthest thing from the lives we were living but still out there waiting for us, the great "eventually," the great "inevitably." Of course we had more important things to do first, or that was the party line. We had our *careers*.

Was it a defensive act, our busy-ness? All those photos of how full and rich and happy our lives were, as if to say, *See, we're fine without children.* Quick, someone plan a dinner party or a weekend upstate before we start squinting at our boyfriends, wondering if they'd meet us halfway.

I would have said that it was with morbid curiosity that I spent hours reading the personal blogs of women, usually religious, often Mormon, who had gaggles of children all dressed in J. Crew and eating pancakes. Their lives, or what they presented of them, were startlingly simple. They seemed to do nothing but cook and clean and go on photogenic outings with their large families, all of them wearing spotless clothing. Their inner lives, or what they shared of them, could be broken down into a few themes and always included gratitude for all of God's blessings and the desire to slow down and be more present so they could better enjoy their precious time with their precious families. Oh, and their desire to have more babies.

After a couple of years of obsessively reading these women's blogs (ironically, I told myself), I began to see the appeal of their ethos. None of this deciding-how-you-feel-about-marriage crap. No weighing options, no making your case to a boyfriend who wasn't sure if he wanted to get married. No putting off babies to the very last minute, no pretending you didn't care, no playing it cool for so long you didn't even remember how to have real desire, real hope. These women, the dreaded mommy bloggers, at least knew what they wanted. They had a clear path, while my friends and I were looking at videos of their babies on our phones and handing them to our boyfriends, who rolled their eyes but—"I swear!"—cracked smiles. It would be all I thought about for a week, how he'd smiled at the video of a baby, and what did that mean?

Instead of asking direct questions—too risky—we took moments like these as signs, played them on loops in our heads, dissected them over drinks. If this was childish, it was a cultural childishness, that of the ambitious young woman too smart for her own good. We were city dwellers, and we were dating (if you could call it that) in a pool of men who always had other, better options. There was always someone younger, someone who expected less. We knew how to play it, how not to need anything. We could almost convince ourselves. Most of us swore we were not interested in having children, and those who might be were supposed to act blasé about the idea. The only acceptable response other than "God, no" to the question of wanting children was "Oh, maybe someday." Wanting to have a baby was a desperate quality in a woman, like wanting a relationship multiplied by a thousand, and it got more desperate with age. The possibility of ending up alone was always there, in the background. My friends and I all took turns being convinced it would be reality, with varying degrees of acceptance. Being alone in New York didn't seem so bad—exhausting, maybe, but stimulating, always something to do, someone to see. But admitting you wanted a baby—and wanted the pancakes and the maternity clothes and the chubby spawn around a table—and then not getting it because it just didn't pan out? That was too much, too cruel. Better to try for things more within your control: Better jobs, nicer apartments. Enviable vacations. Better to shrug and say, "Maybe someday."

(Except for Sara. Sara says she genuinely doesn't want to have children, and we believe her. I envy her decisiveness. She *knows*.)

The problem was that with every year of being by ourselves, of moving forward with work, of getting used to our freedom, of learning how to be happy, we got closer to needing to have a baby (*Time's up!*) and completely upending the lives and selves we'd been building.

Only at our lowest and most confessional, or our most conspiratorial, did we acknowledge that we had a deadline. If one of our childhood friends had just announced a pregnancy on Facebook, or if one of our moms reminded us she'd had three kids by the time she was twenty-nine, or if one of us was ovulating and had just run into an ex who was married now? Then we got worried. Then we started looking up fertility statistics and how much it cost to freeze your eggs. Other days, days when we saw a woman trying to carry a stroller up the subway steps or heard that a woman we were jealous of had just moved to Paris or published a book or bought a house or gotten a divorce, well, then we were still young, had so much living to do. Why ruin things now, just when they were getting good?

We told one another we had till we were thirty-eight but privately thought thirty-five. If you wanted more than one kid—and who would dare to be so greedy—well, best to start at thirty-three. Just don't share this out loud. Life math, years counted out on fingers across from one another in bars and diner booths in big cities across America, dictated that you needed a year or two of marriage before you had kids so you could "enjoy life as a married couple," which felt as compulsory as it was made up. Pregnancy was ten months. Everyone *said* nine but we knew better. Our expertise on the subject of pregnancy was a dead giveaway of our private preoccupation, much as we'd disavow it. A year to plan a wedding (though, if necessary, six months)...and there we were, back at our current age. Twenty-eight. *Fuck.*

Before we left the bar, Lindsay showed us the programs for her wedding that Brian had designed and we oohed and aahed. "I just hope I'll be able to drink for it," I said gravely, and she shot me a look. "I'm not trying to steal your thunder, I promise," I said, mostly joking.

"Unless you give birth *at* my wedding reception, you won't, don't worry."

Halle and Sara made faces into their drinks and I laughed.

When we said our good-byes, Halle called after me, "Take a test, dude!"

"I will, I swear!"

I woke up the next morning feeling hungover from the one beer I'd drunk, and when I went to the bathroom I found blood in my underwear. *So Lindsay was right,* I thought. *It was just stress after all.* I put in a tampon and went for a run in the park.

Later that night I felt for the tampon string, yanked it out, went to wrap it up in toilet paper, and saw that it was blank, not a trace of blood. Confused, I put in another one and went to sleep. In the morning, still nothing. This had never happened before. My period had never started to say something and then taken it back. Where was the rest of it? I waited and waited. This was new. This was unprecedented. This was some coy shit.

By Wednesday my period still hadn't come back, and I was getting no real work done. I was fed up with myself. I couldn't live in the uncertainty any longer. I stood up from my desk and went out the door.

I headed down the block in twilight just as people with day jobs who got out at a decent hour were pouring out of the subway stations. Dustin would be home at seven from his book-marketing job and would be up late working after we had dinner. Our life did not look like I thought it would when we had a baby, someday, that was for sure. We didn't own a home, or a car. I didn't even have health insurance. We lived in a railroad apartment; there were doorways but no doors, just one long, narrow rectangle. The bathroom had no sink, the ceiling was caving in, and the linoleum on the kitchen floor peeled up in more than one place. There was no extra room where a baby could live; there were no rooms at all, really.

I was not a *writer*-writer. I was editing a personal-finance blog part-time for a thousand dollars a month and living off dumb-luck money I'd gotten when an internet company I worked for when I was twenty-four was acquired by Yahoo.

I crossed the street to the drugstore. It felt foolish to say, *Let's have a baby!* Imagine the optimism. I had wanted a baby the way you want things you can't have, dreams you know you won't pursue, or not yet. Like, *One day, when we open a restaurant,* or *One day, when we live in an Airstream trailer,* or *One day, when we make artisanal caramels on a goat farm.* Dustin and I had a lot of these. I was ashamed to want a baby, to be that sort of woman. And, worse, to want to bring a child into our barely established lives.

I went through the automatic door of the drugstore, down the fluorescent-lit aisles. I grabbed the most expensive test I could find—$23.99 and digital, advertised as error-proof. I do not intellectually subscribe to the idea that expense is a reliable indicator of quality, but I suppose that when it comes down to it, my gut is ruled by the illusions of capitalism.

PREGNANT

NOT PREGNANT

It wasn't just the phrasing that made me want it to say yes. *Pregnant* meant new and different; *pregnant* meant we were fucked but maybe in a redeeming way. *Pregnant* meant throwing up our hands, giving ourselves over to fate, doing something crazy. It seemed romantic, reckless, wild, like packing up all our stuff and going on a long trip with no itinerary. For twenty years. No, for forever.

When Dustin got home from work I gestured toward the pink box on our bed (*Know five days sooner!*) then walked away, embarrassed, feeling a sort of pregnancy-test impostor syndrome. Like, *Who am I to be taking this?* It looked like a set piece in someone else's life.

"Ooh, hoo-hoo," he said, kissing me hello.

I tried not to smile. I tried to conjure some dread. "I'll

take it in the morning," I announced. "Supposedly that's when it's most accurate."

"Really?"

"Yeah. You know. When your pee is the most... potent."

Dustin gave me a funny look and shrugged. I wanted to prolong the ambiguity for reasons I couldn't quite articulate, like when you want dessert but don't order it at a restaurant—self-denial as reflex. I was all worked up, dying to know but also wanting to spend one more night as not-a-mother.

When Dustin woke up to pee the next morning, I told him to check the test that I'd peed on and left on the back of the toilet without looking at it. I was hiding under the covers.

"It says *pregnant,*" he called from the bathroom.

"No!" I said.

"Yup," he said, laughing. He was standing there in American Apparel underwear, shirtless, leaning in the doorway and holding the test with a strange casualness, like it was a cigarette or his toothbrush and not a harbinger of things to come.

"No!" I shouted. "No!"

"Well, that's what it says." He came over to me, pulled off the blankets, and kissed me hard. Before we let the news settle in, he pulled off my underwear and then his and we had rushed, crazed sex. He didn't stop to rustle around for a condom, didn't pull out and come on my stomach. I was pregnant. We came at the same time and then collapsed. We both stared at the ceiling.

Breakfast was quiet. I was in his T-shirt feeling a brand-new sort of bodily vulnerability, like what if a spider crawled up my leg and up my birth canal and bit the baby?

"Are you freaking out?" I asked.

"No," he said, and he gestured for me to come sit in his lap. Quiet tears streamed down my face.

"Don't freak out!" I said when he left for work. He waved without turning around, walked down the hall with his bike on his shoulder. I got back in bed, took out my laptop, and immediately chatted Halle.

Hiiiiiiii.

Did you take a test?

Yep.

?????

YEP.

We met on the corner of my block ten minutes later. She held out her arms as I walked up to her. "Congratulations, dude! You're going to be a great mom."

I pulled away. "Ha, no, I don't know. I don't know what we're gonna do."

I told her the story on our way to Enid's, a restaurant in the center of our neighborhood where we had been meeting to catch up since we first moved to the city. I went through all the details: how Dustin reacted, what I said, how I felt, and then we sat down at a booth.

"Okay," she said. "Obviously you are going to have the baby but I am totally willing to humor you by having this debate."

An hour later, after we had talked about money, about health care, about my grad-school applications, about changing my wedding date, we were back on the sidewalk in search of prenatal vitamins. Buying them without Dustin there with me felt like a minor betrayal. "But if we do have the baby, we want it to have a spine, right?" Halle and I giggled in the aisles of Duane Reade. Part of me loved this feeling of being steamrolled by life, of being totally fucked. I was rueful, ready to lie down. It *was* funny, wasn't it, to face something this big? To go through with something that was so clearly a bad idea?

"I guess I should cancel my Weight Watchers subscription!" I said to Halle when we were back out on the street, my contraband in a plastic bag around my wrist. I was flinging it around, letting it hit my thigh, like a small child.

"Yea-ah!" she said.

"It's fucking eighteen dollars a month!" I said. "Fuck you, patriarchy!" We laughed, darkly. I'd finally managed to jettison my lifelong desire to lose ten pounds. All it took was getting pregnant. Unfortunately, that also meant giving birth and raising a child, trading one set of impossible societal expectations for another.

"I should go work," I told Halle, still laughing in disbelief. "I need to get some writing done today." As if I weren't going to go sit in the library and panic-Google for the next five hours.

How much do babies cost per year
"I regret having my child"
abortion new york city
best time to have a baby
baby age 29
writing career, baby
cost of birth without health insurance new york city
writer mother new york city

"Okay," Halle said, hugging me again. "I love you. I'm excited!"

"Love you too," I said, weak, tired. "Thanks for meeting me."

"Of course, dude!" she said, all Midwestern sweetness. "Just one thing, though—"

"Yeah?"

"I support you no matter what you do, but if you do have the baby, you have to let me throw the gender-reveal party."

"We are *not* going to have a fucking gender-reveal party!" I yelled after her.

I sat down at the library just like I'd been doing every day for weeks. I didn't write a word.

That night I met Dustin in a church basement after he got off work. Not to pray but to pick up our CSA farm share. We stood in front of crates of late-summer tomatoes and zucchini, solemn. We'd been playing house for years and the universe had called our bluff. I thought of us lugging a newborn down the steps, tried to imagine carrying all these vegetables and a baby too. No, we would skip next year. Or we wouldn't have the baby. One or the other.

"I talked to Amy today," I said. "She says she got an abortion on the Upper East Side."

"Yeah?" he said. "And you had this talk out of nowhere, huh?"

He was smiling. He looked relieved.

I rolled my eyes, threw tomatoes in a tote bag. "Anyway, she said they put her to sleep and when she woke up, she was sitting in a big armchair. Then she ate cookies. Then she left."

"Cookies, eh? Were they good cookies?"

I looked at him. "What do you mean?"

"What?"

What I was feeling then was subconscious but undeniable. I rushed through pears and flowers and up the steps of the church basement, back out into the September air. I was full of rage, even though I'd brought it up. The hysterical pregnant woman already. I had been trying to appear reasonable, to be (or appear to be) open to his preferences, as if having a baby were like choosing where to order takeout from. *Whatever you want!*

When Dustin caught up to me he had a tote bag over each arm, bayonets of kale poking out from under his armpits. We walked in stride, in perfect weather. The sun was starting to set, doing pretty, atmospheric things. It made me want to put sad music on in my headphones and walk around feeling like the protagonist of my own life.

"Well, for me," he said, "to me, and of course my opinion only counts so much, but I just don't know why we would do it when we aren't ready."

Something sank in me. His reaction was logical but somehow I hadn't anticipated it—it seemed impossible that we could love each other and yet feel so different, *want* such different things. I realized that he had been at work all day feeling fine because he figured we weren't going to go through with it. Was that why he'd insisted he wasn't freaking out? I had managed to talk to all of my friends that day in the library, everyone but him. "You have so much time," Amy had said. Then again, she'd told me she still did the math to see how old her kid would be. She didn't regret it, no, but how could you not think about it from time to time? How could you not do the math? *Loss* was the word that stuck with me.

I told myself that I was willing to get an abortion for him. Of course I was. Right? That's what a reasonable person would say. *I don't want to have a baby with you if you don't want one.* Wasn't that what people said on TV? Didn't I feel that way? I wanted to have a baby with him, and I wanted him to want the same. If he didn't want it, I wanted him to convince me that I didn't either. I wanted to be swayed. I didn't want to have to argue on behalf of my desire.

"We know we want a kid eventually," he said. "In a couple of years we can have one."

"But isn't that kind of dumb? To be like, *Well, we want you but not yet. Sorry, the timing is off.* I mean, isn't this bigger than that?"

"Come on. We can have this baby again in a couple of years."

"This baby?" My voice broke. He was a stranger to me now, my mortal enemy with pesticide-free produce slung over his shoulder. How had I ever loved him at all?

"Yes. This baby. Our baby. In a couple of years. After we travel. When we have more money. Once we are married. We can do it again! It will be the same baby."

I laughed out loud. "Dustin," I said. "That's literally what it won't be, this particular baby." This was weirdly unlike him; he was normally correcting *my* magical thinking.

"I'm just thinking about the money," he said.

I knew he didn't feel like he was in the place in his life he'd imagined he'd be when he had a baby (I didn't either, but wasn't that part of the allure?). He told me later that he'd spent his lunch break crying because he might never get to climb Mount Everest or something like that.

"We can have the baby again in a couple of years," he said again. "When we're ready."

"Stop saying that!" I yelled. I felt like he was being deliberately stupid when he needed to be exactly the opposite. Life was calling for a degree of seriousness we'd never had to summon before. We walked the rest of the way home without talking. I hung back just behind him, not wanting to fall apart on the street.

We had just that week hung up a map that he'd drawn of the entire world, outlined in charcoal, and we were sticking pins in all the places we wanted to go. The plan, our plan, was to get married in early spring, buy two around-the-world plane tickets, and use my Yahoo money to travel for four months before I started grad school. I'd get my MFA, we'd live on my stipend with low overhead, and, eventually, I'd write books and help Dustin manage our family bookstore. Which is to say that over the next three years, we'd be getting married, then traveling, then I'd be writing.

Anyway, the truth was I'd constructed all of those aggressively lovely, dreamy plans as a distraction from what I really wanted, what it seemed like it wasn't time for yet.

When we finally got home, I unlocked the door, slumped into the kitchen, dropped my sackful of produce, and sobbed, standing in the middle of the room on the peeling linoleum. Dustin was trying to take away my baby, the one I'd tried to be so cool about. The one I'd been afraid to say I wanted. The one we could decidedly not have "again" in a couple of years. He came up behind me and tried to hold me, I think.

I managed to flee the two feet over to the bedroom section of our apartment and crumpled onto the bed. "I don't want to get an abortion," I said. The statement sounded pleading in my head but came out as a snarl.

There was a growing ferocity inside of me as my body, at that very moment, was turning a lump of cells into a slightly more human lump of cells. *You did this!* I roared at him in some corner of my being. *It's happening.* But then I turned to face him and tried to be laid back. I tried to see the big picture. It was as if we were at a board meeting about our lives, like if I could get the hand gestures right, I could communicate with some sort of authority.

"I mean, of course you don't *want* to do it, no one wants to do it. It isn't fair. It sucks," he said.

"Easy for you to say." Another wave of rage washed over

me. There was nowhere to go in our shitty, tiny apartment. Dustin was following me around, reasoning with me, or trying to.

"We have enough money," I said. "The stock money. We have enough money to get by for a couple of years, no matter what. I can get a job. It would be fine. So don't say money. Money isn't the reason."

"I guess to me," he said, "an abortion is like getting a root canal or something—but I know it's your body, and there's the Catholic thing…" He trailed off. I went to cry in the bathroom. It was true, I went to Catholic school until I was thirteen. They gave us little plastic babies when we were in third grade. "This is the size of an aborted child at eleven weeks," they said, or some shit like that. They said the babies could feel pain. Weren't they cute? We all went around school in our plaid uniforms with our plastic children tucked into our breast pockets. At this time, 1993 or so, these tiny fetuses were a lot like the tiny plastic animals we were all obsessed with, the Littlest Pet Shop toys. My friends and I tended to both animals and babies like they were small treasures. My mom was furious when I brought my doll home. "What are you, *pro-choice?*" I shouted at her, then slammed the door of our white minivan. I was eight, maybe nine. A woman came to our class to talk about how her aborted fetuses appeared to her as angels. A lifetime of regret. A mortal sin.

No, it wasn't the Catholic thing. Fuck the Catholic thing. This had nothing to do with any of that, which I not only didn't relate to or agree with anymore but found genuinely damaging. Or was Dustin right? Maybe it was the Catholic thing that gave me pause, conferred this sense of fate, wonder, awe. Maybe it was what kept me from taking better charge of my life. Maybe it was what made me a romantic, made me call the cell-lump a baby in the first place. Maybe it was what made me walk around the world feeling like I was a bad person who didn't know what she wanted. Or didn't until now.

Now I wanted too much: I wanted keeping it to feel inevitable, like fate, but also, somehow, for it to be a choice. I wanted to feel trapped and free. I was desperate for there to be a best course of action, some objective truth. I wanted to know what the right thing was; it felt so important to know the right decision, anything to avoid having to make it myself. Was that the most childish part? I couldn't have all of those things and also the baby. I would have to be vulnerable, to recognize my desire and say it out loud.

My truest feelings about the baby began and ended with *I want it.* It was inside of me and I wanted it, and I knew I could take care of it, but for some reason that counted for only so much. I tried to shut out that part of me. That was the hysterical woman in me. That was the baby fever. That was purely hormonal; ridiculous. That was shit you were supposed to transcend when you were a smart woman. When you were a woman in New York City. When you were a woman with ambitions that ran as deep as your feelings, you were supposed to trust the ambitions, not the feelings. You were supposed to plot it out beforehand, talk it over with your other smart friends, follow influential people on Twitter, ask the right ones out for drinks, make daring moves—ascend, ascend, ascend.

A baby is never a particularly good idea, practically speaking, and a baby was an especially bad idea for us. That could have—should have, maybe—been the end of it, the objective truth I was after, but did I have it in me to undo something that was already there, something I yearned for, bad idea or no?

I came out of the bathroom and gripped the door of the refrigerator, staring straight ahead. I didn't know what I was doing there, just that it gave me a reason not to look at him.

Our baby was currently the size of a poppy seed.

The off-white refrigerator was at least fifty years old, another reason we were ill equipped to be parents. I stood in front of it pretending I was deeply engaged in doing something other than trying to gather the strength and self-knowledge to get through this conversation. If I fucked it up, if I got it wrong, I wasn't sure what would happen.

I wanted something I didn't want to want, and I wanted Dustin to lend me the courage, the language, the conviction to go through with it despite my fear. I wanted him to hold my hand and tell me what a good mother I'd be, how beautiful I'd be when I blew up like a balloon, how he couldn't wait.

"If we don't have this baby," I said, through snotty tears, "and I won't do it if you don't want to, but if we don't, then I can't...guarantee anything."

"What do you mean, *guarantee*?" Dustin said, scared.

"I just, I don't know what that would do to us," I managed. "I don't know if I would be able to forgive you. I can't promise you I would."

"Well, that's it, then," he said. "Then we're going to do it." He was breathless. "I need a minute," he said and went to the other side of the apartment. He sat on the couch in the dark. We were silent. I took a shower just to be able to close a door.

Holding Patterns (1 to 41.5)

1.

RECURRING PREGNANCY DREAM: I am somewhere all day and suddenly it hits me—I forgot I had a baby. I run to wherever he is (in a car, in a hotel room, at home, on a log flume at an amusement park), but it's always too late.

As I'm on the way to him, my milk dries up. By the time I get there, he's dried up too. He disappears in my arms. In my dreams, the baby's hunger works like this. It's life or death.

I leave him in a minifridge. Lock it closed and go to a conference. By the time I get back, he has turned into a doll. The baby, refrigerated, has turned plastic. (The baby is always a boy in my dreams, though I'm not sure how I know it.)

Sometimes the baby shrinks and slips under my thigh in the passenger seat of a pickup truck. I get carried away in conversation and lean back in my seat, smashing him. He disappears, absorbed into the seams of the seat cushion.

In the shrinking dreams, he's a balloon with the air let out. I try to feed him anyway but soon he's smaller than my nipple. Soon he is too small to be held with my fingers. I drop him in the grass and he's lost.

I drop him in a big pot of soup. I confuse him with a hot dog and eat him.

Sometimes he morphs into a worm, a snake, the monster in *Dune*. All teeth, all suck. These dreams, where it's me who is consumed by him, me who is destroyed and not vice versa, are a nice respite.

2.

The sickness hits me with impeccable timing—as soon as we decide to keep the baby. It is the worst hangover of my life. I can only lie perfectly still and moan. I don't throw up. That would be too much of a relief.

A few hours in, I feel like jumping ship. I look up at Dustin with tears in my eyes and say, "Maybe this was a mistake." He thinks I am faking my misery, or at least exaggerating it. I can tell. When I confront him he says, "No, I

don't think you're faking it. I just think it's psychosomatic."
As if there's a difference.

3.

I spend my days now half working and half reading about fetal development. Even when I don't have questions I search *pregnancy* [x] *weeks* and read every piece of branded content I can find.

"The patterning of his scalp has begun, though his locks aren't recognizable yet. He's even started growing toenails!"

"His eyes are finally working too, making small side-to-side movements and perceiving light (although the eyelids are still sealed). Peekaboo!"

"Amazingly, your baby's toes and fingers will form their own unique patterns this week as they develop the fingerprints that will stay with them for the rest of their lives."

Each website compares the baby to produce that is suspiciously different. On one website, the baby is a pea pod. On another, at the same number of weeks, a peach. Later there are leeks, radishes, pumpkins, watermelons. I choose to "believe" whichever site makes him sound bigger, more real. I click ahead to the future weeks, feeling a small rebellious thrill.

There are only so many ways I can trace my finger over

this strange in-between period. To revel in my new world. One day I'd have a baby, but for now I was in a holding pattern. Something was *about* to happen. *Pregnancy eight weeks. Nine. Ten. Twelve.* I knew everything there was to know except none of it was particularly useful, none of it an answer to the bigger questions: What will it be like? How will it change me?

4.

Dustin has a publishing conference in Chicago, where my mom lives, so I tag along. Our first morning in town, my mom teaches me to keep a packet of saltines on the bedside table and not get up without eating a few. "The key is to never, ever let your stomach get empty," she says and I nod, feeling like a child. Hunger feels risky now, even dangerous. The second it strikes, I imagine the embryo halting its growth, whirling around with a panicked look in its eyes. I imagine it like a plant, wilting and turning brown.

I feel elderly, half buckled over all day, shuffling down the street with a ginger tea. My mom, however, is glowing.

"Maybe I'll have a miscarriage," I say to my mom offhandedly in the car on our way to an overpriced baby-clothing store that she's insisted on taking me to. She bursts out laughing.

"What?" I say. "I'm only seven weeks. You never know."

"No, honey," she says, shaking her head, giving me a look.

"People have miscarriages *all the time*," I say. "It's a thing that happens." At this point, the pregnancy ending was more comprehensible than it continuing. We'd be heartbroken, then maybe relieved. I'd apply to grad school.

"I know it happens. And you should pray to God that it doesn't because it would be horrible. Horrible."

"Did you ever?"

"Nope," she says, staring over the steering wheel. I sink back into the passenger seat and sigh.

5.

The day that we get home from Chicago we decide, or re-decide, once and for all, to keep the pregnancy. "It's real." "We're doing it." "Okay!" We have urgent, tearful sex and when I go to the bathroom after, I'm bleeding. Ever since I took the pregnancy test, I've been religiously checking the toilet paper for blood, surprised every time it wasn't there. When I see it now, it's almost like my checking made it happen.

I come out of the bathroom and collapse onto Dustin's chest. *I'm bleeding,* I tell him. He starts crying too.

I read articles on my phone and report back that some

bleeding after sex is normal, that it's just that my cervix is newly sensitive. We're relieved but harrowed. At the mercy of something now.

6.

We meet Dustin's sister at the bar down the block from us—called, appropriately, Mother's—to tell her we're having a baby. After hugging us and gasping and saying congratulations, she's quiet for a minute.

"Well, I'm excited!" she says, declaring it.

We laugh and perform exaggerated gestures of relief—Dustin loosens an imaginary necktie.

"Oh, stop," she says, waving at us. Then she gets serious. "I don't feel sorry for you," she says in her definitive, careful, sincere way. "This is a good thing."

"Huh," we say, taking it in like a verdict. So we aren't teenagers after all. We aren't confessing to something.

7.

Lindsay's wedding is in Charleston, South Carolina, and I am eight weeks pregnant. The night before the wedding, my friends stay up late drinking and catching up, and I sit on the couch, sober, answering their questions. Am I excited? Scared? Do I want to get the epidural or try to have a natural birth? "Modern medicine exists for a reason," Sara says. I shrug. I've been reading a book called *Spiritual Midwifery* and want a hippie childbirth, one where no scary needles come near your spine and you can brag to all your friends about it later. I don't say this, though. "We'll see how it goes," I say. "I've never given birth before."

The conversation soon turns to horror stories. Episiotomies gone wrong. Someone's aunt had a dozen corrective surgeries on her perineum. She just had another procedure last year.

"How old are her kids?" I say, trying to sound casual.

"Oh, her youngest is twenty-three."

I blink, trying to get rid of the images flashing in my brain: red, slippery vagina skin ripping in two like a torn bedsheet.

8.

My prenatal yoga teacher has never had a baby herself but somehow this only lends her more authority—it's as if her perspective is unsullied by her own experience. She paces around the studio holding a skeletal model of a woman's pelvis.

"When you're pregnant," she explains to us with a perfect balance of sympathy and matter-of-factness, "sometimes your body changes faster than your awareness of your body."

"Yes!" I say without thinking as I thrust out my hips in a lunge.

I love her, this reassuring woman who never wears a bra and who sways around the studio like a cat—a cat with her nipples out.

9.

Before bed I read Dustin statistics in an official-sounding voice as a way to broach the subject. "*Postpartum Progress* estimates that fifteen percent of new moms get postpartum depression, or one in seven." I break character and look over at him meaningfully.

"Wow," he says, then puts down whatever novel he's reading and gives *me* a meaningful look, like, *Is there something you want to talk about?* "That's a lot of people."

"Yeah," I say. Then I continue: "Women who are prone to mood swings or are affected by birth control or premenstrual syndrome are more likely to suffer from postpartum depression."

"Welp."

"I know. I'm basically guaranteed to get it."

"Okay. So we know to look out for it."

I nod and then go to sleep that night feeling proud, mature, prepared.

10.

One impetuous afternoon in my early pregnancy, after we told our close friends and family but before we told the internet, I find myself alone in the kitchen standing sideways in front of the camera on my laptop. I am supposed to be working but instead decide it is time to post a cryptic photo of my torso to Instagram. The photo doesn't include my face, just my stomach pooching out a little. I caption the photo *Does this shirt make me look pregnant, y/n?* and feel a rush of adrenaline as I hit Post. The comments range from *Ummm* to *What????*

I have reached the agreed-upon threshold—twelve weeks—but posting it on Facebook feels too fraught, like I am conducting a press conference on behalf of my fetus and I might get the tone wrong.

After the first hesitation, the first failed grasp for a new language or, better, a new way of being, I start to understand why people use borrowed phrases: "excited to announce"— like a business acquisition. I want to say it quickly, to get the information out there and over with so that everyone can leave some screaming emoji comments and I can move on to talking about it constantly. I want to have already said it.

11.

Prenatal yoga is a lot like regular yoga except the teacher talks about Kegels and has us walk around grabbing our pubic bones just to get us thinking about them. The new utility of our private parts.

At the beginning of class we sit in a circle in the large, bright room, perched on yoga blocks and blankets, everyone barefoot and shifting lazily. We all go around and say how far along we are and share one thing that's bothering us that week: hip pain, heartburn, can't sleep, sore tits, exhaustion, nausea, deep regret.

Whoever is the most pregnant wins. At eleven weeks, twelve weeks, thirteen, I am apologetic, a chubby impostor, merely bloated. Each body is a revelation. I wish I could put the women nearing forty weeks behind glass and ogle them properly. As it is, I spend most of my mental energy trying to sneak glances at their popped-out belly buttons between warrior poses. They all seem to have the same faraway look, one that makes me feel a sort of naive adoration. Looking at them is like looking into the future.

12.

The sonograms are sacred things. My obstetrician runs one each time I visit her and I always hold my breath, brace myself for bad news. I want her to do the ultrasound, of course, to flip the switch that turns on the machine and ask me to yank my leggings down around my hips.

I've never quite loved my doctor, my ob-gyn, but I've been going to her for years and the idea of finding a new one is overwhelming. When I complain about her, Dustin gently reminds me we could switch, that it's worth the trouble, but I get defensive and change the subject. There's so much about this that's unfamiliar. I don't want one more new thing.

My palms sweat while Dr. R. tries to find the baby's heartbeat, and the hygienic paper crinkles when I grip it, steeling myself for tragedy. I can't see how anyone could go looking for a heartbeat without the sinking feeling it won't be there, but the doctor just clucks her tongue when she can't find it right away and says the baby is being stubborn. I'm so filled with dread I don't even laugh politely, feeling the resignation of an anxious person buckling in for a transatlantic flight.

Then the relief when we touch down. Implausibly, improbably, defying all hunches, the baby is there, darting like a guppy in his black-and-white home.

13.

He was only ever real for the afternoons and evenings after an ultrasound. I'd push open the doors to the sight of yellow cabs and buses rushing by along Central Park, then pace around the sidewalk texting my vital signs and images of the printed-out sonogram photos.

Friends text back: So, what am I seeing here?

On one such jubilant afternoon, the fetus and I passed by the Museum of Natural History and I decided we should go in. I stood under the giant whale and cried, full of awe, thinking, *You are going to come here one day. We are going to come here together.*

14.

I rush around the apartment grabbing my stuff so I can make it to yoga class on time, but I stop short of the door and stand a few feet in front of Dustin, who is sitting at the table eating toast. He beckons me over to him but I stay where I am and tug at my shirt.

"Do I look pregnant today?" I turn sideways for the full effect.

"Meaghan," he says, trying not to laugh at me, "you look pregnant every day. You *are* pregnant."

15.

Were other women changed immediately? Did they become mothers the minute they peed on a stick and went screaming down the hallway? Or was it like the time I was in first grade and came home from school crying to my mother because all the kids knew how to read but me?

"Nobody knows how to read yet," my mom assured me. "That's why you're in school. To learn!"

"No, Mom!" I told her. I was insistent. "They do. I can tell because during silent reading time everyone looks at the pages of their books and moves their lips."

"Oh," she said. "Well, what do you do?"

"I look at the pages of my book and move my lips!"

16.

When my mom visits for Thanksgiving, I am sixteen weeks pregnant and just starting to show. Halfway into an afternoon of shopping with her and Dustin, I'm convinced I feel something wet in my underwear. I keep this information to myself at first and shuffle down the block, twisting this way and that to get to the bottom of it. I consider trying on some clothes just so I can be alone in a dressing room, stick a hand down my underwear, and assess the damage. Dustin and my mom stop to get a coffee and I tell them I want to use the bathroom. *This is it,* I think, the moment of truth. There is a long line and when they wander over with their drinks to see what's taking so long, I look up at them and start crying. "I think I feel blood," I confess. Everyone turns white. When I come back from the bathroom, I'm somber. I shake my head a quick no; it was nothing.

This scene plays out around once a week.

The next time it happens, my mom has had enough. "Baby, you have to stop reading everything you can find! You know too much! You're going to drive yourself crazy," she says. "This was not how it was in our day, and you know what, I think it was better that way."

I don't tell her about the stillbirth memoir I just bought at the bookstore a week earlier. Or that I have the New York City tenancy laws about lead paint committed to memory.

17.

I spent most of my life being just a little bit fat and always figured that pregnancy would be a nice reprieve. I imagined I would fall in love with my body and feel ready to pose for pictures in Facebook updates. I had this image in my mind of how I'd look pregnant, mostly based on the type of woman who posed on lifestyle blogs and looked "like a beanpole that swallowed a bowling ball."

My whole life, I've had upper arms I've wanted to hide in a cardigan, but for some reason in this image of myself as a pregnant woman, my arms and legs are long and thin, set off by a perfectly round midsection. Like maybe as my belly grew, the rest of me would look smaller? In my fantasies I am hugging my large stomach and wearing some sort of flowing, floral vintage dress. I am emanating effortless joy.

When have I ever willingly posed for, to use dating-app parlance, a full-body shot? When have I ever said, *Here is my body, please look at it while I stand here smiling, and take a picture so we can remember it always.*

I should be able to wear tight dresses, things that under normal circumstances would reveal too much of my gut. Now, I remind myself, my gut is a source of pride. Now my gut is a miracle. I know I am supposed to enjoy that, and on certain days, in certain outfits, I do manage to float along in cotton jersey with an undeniable sense of well-being. Other times, in other outfits, I'm chiefly concerned that people will assume I'm just fat.

Some days, when I catch sight of myself, an automatic, self-hating part of my brain still recoils, still thinks, *Bad.* My body is jutting where it should not jut. There's no hiding it.

18.

The first time a man offers me his seat on the subway, my face gets hot. He stands up in a crowded car and gestures, grandly, toward his still-warm space. I smile; I'd like to sit but find myself demurring reflexively, feeling put on the spot and wanting the whole interaction to end. I wave my hand at him, shaking my head. *No. It's fine.* He insists. I say no. I feel a train car's worth of eyes on me, the pregnant lady, blushing and breaking into a sweat.

19.

When the radiology tech says, "Okay! It's a boy," Dustin, sitting off in the dark, holding my outstretched hand, goes, "Huh," without affect.

All we had really imagined was a girl. We both had sisters only. Even the family dogs I had growing up were girls. What was a boy?

20.

The day we find out the baby is a boy is the day I first feel him, or feel *something*. It's not a kick; more like a vibration—a phone buzzing, briefly, inside of me. It's wild to feel a brand-new sensation in a place where nothing has stirred before. It feels like being tapped on the shoulder from the inside. *I exist, I exist, I exist.*

21.

For Christmas we drive the ten hours to Michigan from New York, splitting the cost of a rental car with Dustin's sister and dad. I am hungry the whole time but feel sheepish about it. I don't know how to speak up: *Feed me, I'm having your grandchild.*

What kind of mother can't do this for herself? I cry quietly in the backseat, feeling inadequate and desperately needing to piss.

When we get there, I'm presented with my own Christmas stocking, embroidered by my not-yet-mother-in-law, who also brings out Dustin's baby book. In it we find a carbon copy of her birth story, which was written on a typewriter in 1982. She gave birth to him without an epidural, at a birth center under dim lights. They put him directly in a warm bath. I feel cowed. I tell her about all the yoga I've been doing.

My own mother had me via C-section after I got stuck in her birth canal for hours. It was Friday the thirteenth and the on-call anesthesiologist had been locked in a tennis court as a prank. She had my younger sister two years later without drugs, she tells me, but when I talk on the phone to my dad, whom she's been divorced from for a decade, he snickers and tells me she got the epidural.

22.

The day after we get to Michigan, I e-mail my friend Anna, who wants to know how I'm holding up. I tell her not so good. Allergies, hunger, rage. After reading my missive out loud to her mother, Anna transcribes her mom's advice for me:

She should tell people what she needs and they should do it for her. If she needs something and she's pregnant she should get it. That's what I think. She has a kind of authority as a pregnant person that she should learn to use because the minute the baby arrives, she will a) fall in love, like she'd never been in love before, but b) she will have a new and impetuous boss.

I know she's right. The authority of the pregnant person. I can see that it's there in the way people treat me, in their endless questions and concern. But I don't feel it in myself at all. "How are you feeling?" everyone asks me, and every time I'm taken aback. I feel dumbstruck. Unwieldy. Overwhelmed.

23.

In the privacy of our rental car the next morning, I tell Dustin I'm worried. I haven't felt the baby move, not since that one time back in New York before we left. I keep waiting and waiting, but nothing. When he waves my fear away like he always does, I lose it.

"I haven't felt him at all! I can't feel anything!" I yell at him while he's driving. *"The baby is dead!"* I scream the scream of a woman who is not being taken seriously, who is not being fed enough, coddled enough, who is not being ultrasounded every hour so that she can be reassured that the possible is not probable, is not inevitable. A vein in my forehead feels like it's going to pop and my throat aches with urgency as I watch Dustin's face change from what looks like rage to pity—his lunatic fiancée, all of her hormones.

"It's fine, baby, I know he's fine. I know it," Dustin says, finally crying. "We just have to get through this week. We have the next appointment when we get home." This means nothing to me, but just seeing that I've shaken him is something. What I really want him to acknowledge, to feel with me, is that we are standing at the precipice of death now all the time. That it's undeniable, part of the deal sooner or later, inextricable from life. We created a death. And how could he not take that seriously?

He holds my hand and then my stomach, and we keep dri-

54

ving down the bleak Michigan highway. The trees are covered in icicles, which look menacing to me, dangling in the wind.

24.

Back home in New York just after the new year, we go to our anatomy-scan ultrasound. Our son is pronounced perfect, twenty-one weeks old, definitely a boy. They ration out this information to us in offhanded remarks: "See, this is his skull from above." Is it? All my fear seems foolish now. I replace it with hope. Helpless, dumbfounded, uncertain hope.

25.

I am too shy to talk to the baby out loud. I feel goofy when I creep over to his dresser to fold and refold his baby clothes. Dustin makes fun of me. I roll my eyes but wish he would leave and let me do this in private.

26.

As soon as we found out we were having a boy, I knew we were screwed, name-wise. Naming a girl would have been hard enough, but girls' names are lovely, myriad. I spent my whole life dreaming them up. A boy? I hadn't given it any thought.

Dustin and I sit in restaurants writing names on paper tablecloths. We take turns hating and then preferring names, reminding each other that given our genes, this baby will inevitably grow up to be chubby and bespectacled. We have to be careful.

When we do settle on an idea, we see and hear it everywhere, in baby catalogs and in the mouths of women at Baby Gap shopping for their nephews. It sounds so unspecial, no longer ours, so we cross it off the list, not wanting to be—God forbid—clichéd in this, our most significant display of personal taste.

I picture our baby's name floating somewhere just beyond my consciousness, like when you forget a word and know that as soon as you stop trying to remember, it will come to you. Except in this case, it doesn't. I find I'm left with the same old words I had before, the same short list of names worn thin by the lives of other men.

"We'll figure it out," I tell Dustin. "We work best under pressure." I hope it's true.

27.

Sometimes I forget it entirely, that I'm pregnant. I sit for hours at a coffee shop writing, and my condition slips my mind. These are good days, days when I feel like I'm liberated, just a brain floating in a vat.

But the spell is broken when I stand up to go to the bathroom and try to squeeze past the necks of young Brooklyn coffee-shop men, my new stomach grazing the tips of their ears. "Sorry, sorry!" Everyone turns and sees my conspicuous body. I am a stranger who is pregnant. In this way I make more sense to them than I do to myself.

28.

By the time I am twenty-eight weeks pregnant, my baby is the size of an eggplant and I've learned that *heartburn* is the perfect name for heartburn—it feels like burping fire.

At prenatal yoga I have leveled up into truly pregnant. Hugely pregnant. Downward dog is no longer a possibility for me. I do all of the hands-and-knees stuff with my elbows on blocks. It feels right to be this incapacitated.

The best days—rare—are the days when my bigness feels like grandeur as I drag myself down the street.

29.

I worry I am not "savoring my pregnancy." There is always something I feel like I should be doing, some excitement I should be stoking—not just in myself but in everybody else too. It's my role, I suspect, to be a sort of spiritual leader, the matriarch in our church of anticipation.

I should be journaling, blogging, documenting my moods and cravings, and updating my registry. There should be Polaroids our son finds in a shoe box thirty years from now and feels sentimental about. I want this baby to think his mom was radiant, effortlessly so, hugging her massive, miraculous body in floral prints. I want him to post them to the 2045 version of Instagram. I want his friends to leave comments about my fashion sense.

30.

No one believes us when we say we have no idea what to name the baby.

"Oh, so you're keeping it a secret?" they say. "What are you deciding between?" Others seem to think we're being difficult on purpose.

"Well," I venture on a night out with friends, "we call him Gus, kind of as a joke, but it's starting to feel like it's actually his name." Sharing this feels embarrassing and too vulnerable, like talking about a novel before you start writing it.

"*Gus?*" I look up to see Halle visibly recoiling. "You can't name him that!" she says, then catches herself. "Well, you can do whatever you want. I'm sure we'd come around to it. But I'll be honest. I hate it."

"Hey, what about William? That's cute, right?"

"Bill, though?" I picture a little baby in wire-framed glasses and a blue oxford shirt.

We like Cal but it sounds weak and also somehow like a bully. David is okay but Dave sounds like he puts too much gel in his hair. I dated a Charlie and he wore his cell phone on his belt. Toby sounds like his collar is always wrinkled and folded over on itself. Show me a boy's name and I'll show you a man who has ruined it.

"What about Arthur? I kinda like that. I don't know any Arthurs."

"Oh, actually, a friend of mine was going to name her baby that."

"Yeah?"

"Yes. But she didn't because her husband pointed out that everyone would call him Farty Artie."

31.

A woman at the farmers' market says, "Are you... pregnant?" with hesitation and it upsets me.

"What else would I be?" I say to her. Her uncertainty is confirmation: I am fat everywhere, not just in my sacred belly. To console myself I eat a pint of fancy gelato every single night. Pregnancy makes me feel trapped sometimes, but other times I think, *You'll never be this free again.*

32.

I want to write something meaningful before the baby comes. A novel, preferably. Though I have no ideas and have so far made no moves toward the goal, I'm convinced that if I can just get in deep with a big, ambitious project now, I'll be able to relax and enjoy myself later, when the baby is here. I try explaining this to friends on the train home from dinner, though it's clear I'm making the case more to myself than to them. "Something I can pick up later, in short bursts, you know? So that I won't feel so lost."

"That makes sense!" Lindsay says, nodding with encouragement.

"Though who knows what I'll have time for—"

Lindsay looks down at me from her grip on the subway

pole. "Babies sleep all the time anyway, don't they?" she says. "I'm sure it will be easy enough to get writing done."

I turn away from her, full of dread but not wanting to explain myself. The time after the baby feels like an oblivion, like anything could happen. I don't even know who I will be after him. Then the creeping revelation: If I let him, my son will be the reason I don't do all sorts of things. I'm starting it already.

33.

On a weekday afternoon I walk down the block to the library to work and see a boy who must be ten or eleven dancing alone on the sidewalk outside an apartment building. His pants are pulled up high, his ankles showing. He can't see me coming but I'm not sure he'd care if he did. He twists his body in jerky, strange, wondrous movements. He looks incredibly free, incredibly happy, in his own world. I stop short and then start crying, surprising myself.

I know I will love my son, that somehow I already do, but I haven't been able to imagine what it will be like, how I will love him. I haven't pictured him yet, my funny boy.

34.

My friend Meredith and I haven't seen each other in a long time; for years we've been swearing we'll hang out soon but never do. She has a new baby, and now that we have something in common I find myself on the PATH train to visit her in Hoboken so she can give me advice while she breastfeeds.

I sit on the carpet and listen eagerly to every detail of her victoriously unmedicated labor. She seems happy and open and makes me take a box of her leftover raspberry leaf tea, which she says will strengthen my uterus. She instructs me to buy an exercise ball and sit on it for a few hours every day to help relax my pelvic floor and hands me a copy of something called Hypnobabies, a series of guided meditations on CD. They are meant to hypnotize you into thinking that labor doesn't hurt. Contractions are "surges" and laboring women are strong, capable, relaxed. She tells me it all went out the window once labor started but it was helpful beforehand. *Empowering.*

I leave her apartment feeling grateful and equipped. It feels so good to have a to-do list.

35.

When I get home I open up my laptop to work but instead search *natural childbirth* on YouTube. I hide my face and muffle screams while I watch perineum after perineum stretch to its limits, tiny squashed skulls pushing through and then receding, the husbands just out of frame. The women are moaning and groaning on birthing stools or down on all fours. As the camera zooms in on a slime-covered head coming out of what no longer looks like a vagina, you can hear the midwife lovingly direct the laboring woman: "Catch your baby! Reach down and catch your baby!" *Can't someone else catch the damn baby for her?* I think, but the woman looks down and pulls it, slimy and wet, up to her chest, laughing in disbelief. I cry every time. I laugh too. It's incredible. I wish it weren't going to happen to me, but still. How can you argue with it?

When I stand up from our bed to go to the bathroom that night, Dustin's eyes get wide and he points to my right tit.

I look down to find my white maternity tank top glued to my nipple, a yellow stain where some kind of liquid— colostrum—has oozed out.

"It must have happened when the babies were crying in the videos!" Dustin says, excited. I flee to the bathroom, feeling like a boy who has been caught masturbating.

In the solitary kingdom of our tiny bathroom, I feel queasy but powerful. I hunch over my own body and squint into a mirror the same way I did twenty years ago, on the edge of puberty. Now here I am again. The orchestra of my body has been warming up and I didn't even know it.

36.

Our first childbirth class starts when I am thirty-six weeks pregnant. The teacher opens class by asking us to go around the room and share what we are most afraid of. I make a joke about my mother coming to stay with us but what I'm really thinking about are the bones of the baby's head being squeezed together, the way I'd seen it in the YouTube videos, the plates of his skull overlapping, forming a sickening cone. I'm thinking about my body tearing open to accommodate his in ways I wouldn't be able to see or stop from happening.

I know that to be afraid of birth, to doubt your body's ability to do this "most natural thing in the world," is, according to all of the media I am consuming, a sort of sin. I know this and yet I am still unspeakably afraid. I feel like a small animal. A woman. A failure already.

37.

Dustin has a chart about pain medication he found in his *Birth Partner* book and he tries to go over it with me, but I shut down without meaning to. "Not right now!" I say, and then I start crying. My self-doubt is a failure in and of itself, I know. I try to shake it off. I try listening to the Hypnobabies but find myself unable to turn off the critical part of my brain and really get into it. "Your energy and thoughts about childbirth are now positive and healthy at all times," the woman says in a throaty monotone.

A willing suspension of disbelief seems to be required. As much as I want to believe, as much as I would rather be foolish than scared, I find I can't quite summon it. Every time someone says, "Your body is meant to do this," I think of all the women who used to die in childbirth. All the women who still do.

38.

For childbirth class number two (of four), we do an experiment. Our teacher, a chipper blond woman who has never had a baby, passes around little cups of ice to all of us and then takes her place in front of the room. She announces that we'll be practicing pain management today by holding a piece of ice in our hands—squeezing it—for sixty seconds, about the length of a contraction. We're all joking and a little excited to do the activity. Finally something practical, something to help us feel accomplished, prepared.

Oh, shit, I think as soon as it starts. I want to drop the ice or throw it. Cheating, I move it to different parts of my hand. We have to keep our eyes closed, which only makes it worse. Who knew ice could hurt so much? We are alone with our pain.

After sixty seconds are up, the teacher asks us how it went. *Awful,* I think. "Did it feel longer than sixty seconds?" she asks.

"*Yes!*" I shout to what seems like a leading question, but the people around me, liars all, shake their heads. The teacher asks for more feedback, and one of the dads raises his hand.

"Well, it was like I was aware of the pain but it didn't bother me. I acknowledged it and just sat with it. Time went by quickly."

Fuck you, I think.

Another guy takes the floor. "I did this thing where I listened to the ticking of the clock without counting the seconds. I just embraced the passage of time. It felt really fast."

I laugh out loud at this; I can't help it.

"Wow," our teacher says, "very nice." She's clearly impressed.

I search the room in vain for someone to make eye

contact with, someone to share a knowing eye-roll with. The women, of course, stay quiet. We are already moving inward, already slipping. This is only a peek at the task that lies ahead of us.

I've spent the past eight months trying to think about pain, searching my memory for something to compare it to and coming up short. Menstrual cramps are a popular analog, but to me they seem defined by their dullness. I've never had surgery, can't remember the last time I skinned my knee. When was the last time something really, really hurt, anyway? In all my grasping, I haven't been able to imagine it.

The ice, though—it does the job.

39.

A week after class ends we get an e-mail from our childbirth instructor that's full of exercises and visualizations to try at home: Our pelvic bones opening. The vagina as a flower, also opening. Waves rising and falling as we breathe. She sends us an illustrated pdf of birthing positions and a link to cesarean rates at New York hospitals. These statistics are treated like a warning, a disturbing trend that is up to us to resist. Getting a C-section has become a sort of moral failure in my eyes. I haven't read much of anything about preparing for or recovering from one, convinced that I don't need to know. Ignoring the possibility entirely feels like a way to keep it from happening.

The instructor encourages us to keep practicing with the ice, adding a numbered list of exercises to try.

8: Instead of actively trying to push away the sensation, we make friends with our pain. We get to know it better, get less tense and thus feel less pain. Be utterly curious about it…notice how it changes from moment to moment, notice exactly where it's located, where it begins and ends, try to look into the pain and see what it looks like…imagine you're seeing the feeling under a magnifying glass and slowly studying the edges of the pain…does the feeling have any colors or textures?

40.

When I go for my final prenatal appointment, a week over-due, my doctor writes *Sex* on a prescription pad and hands it to me with a smile. My cervix is "high and tight," she says. Not good right now.

Before I leave, she asks me what we're going to name our son, and I confess to her that we still don't know.

"Waiting to see his face, huh?"

"Yes!" That seems as good a line as any. We'll see the baby's face and be changed by him; we'll feel the conviction we've been waiting for all along. We'll be transformed into people who have convictions. Parents.

41.

I don't do the unthinkable (sex) but I do consider asking Dustin to jerk off into my vagina. This is scientifically sound.

41.5.

When the baby is nine days overdue, and I am forty-one and a half weeks pregnant, it occurs to me that my fear is what is holding him in. Ina May Gaskin, the legendary midwife and author and subject of documentaries I've hungrily consumed, would say that the fear is a "block." If she were here, she'd give me a stern talking-to and send me off to walk in the woods, so Dustin and I go for a hike around the neighborhood. Dustin takes a million pictures. Things feel big. We are two people in love about to have a baby, and we're shuffling down the street arm in arm. I feel tired, sore, claustrophobic. I'm uncomfortable in my own skin, afraid of what's to come. To the untrained eye, though, I am glowing.

A Birth Story

IT WAS MONDAY, June 2, and I was wide awake at six a.m. Maybe to most people—certainly to most parents—this hour doesn't sound remarkable, but for me it was. It was the first day in a lifetime of six-in-the-mornings.

By this point, I was ten days past my due date and I had a very specific and recurring fantasy of being moved around town in a hammock flown by a helicopter. I wanted to be airlifted between boroughs.

When I told Dustin this wish, he was quiet for a second. He had learned to reply with caution, but I imagine in this case he just couldn't help himself.

"Like a whale?" he asked.

I had been waking up "still pregnant" for quite some time—289 days, to be exact. My mom was in town, staying at an Airbnb rental a block away. I was chugging raspberry leaf tea, bouncing on a purple exercise ball whenever I could, shoving evening primrose oil pills up my vagina, paying forty dollars a pop for community acupuncture sessions I didn't believe in, and doing something called "the Labor Dance." The Dance (preferred shorthand) involves rubbing one's belly vigorously in a clockwise direction and then getting as close to twerking as one can at forty-one weeks pregnant.

Now I was wide awake and staring at the wall. Then *ow*. It was like the crest of a period cramp if you have forgotten to take Tylenol. I lay there with my mind racing for a while, then got up and ate Frosted Mini-Wheats, the way I had done for much of my pregnancy. Dustin was sleeping. I felt another one. Another "thing." *Ow*. I got in the shower, jittery with this new development. *Ow-ow-ow*. I grabbed the towel rack and wondered how many more showers I'd take that day. In all of my natural childbirth classes, everyone raved about the magic of hot showers. I suspected, or feared, that their analgesic powers were not as advertised. *Ow*.

I got back into bed and lay there, naked and huge, staring at Dustin sleeping, waiting for him to wake up. I didn't want to look at the clock, but I looked at the clock, and the *ow*s were fifteen minutes or so apart. "Ow, ow, ow," I whispered into my arm. So far the pain was about as bad as a stubbed toe. It was a *Damn!* pain, but it was still amusing. I was proud of it, too, of my body. It had finally kicked itself into gear.

I was also a little excited because I didn't feel like working that day or going to another doctor appointment at the hospital, forty minutes away. The appointments were for overdue women. You sat in a roomful of armchairs upholstered in cornflower-blue material that could be wiped down with a washcloth and you pulled up your shirt to reveal your belly, and the nurse lubed you up and strapped a monitor to you and you sat with the other women whose bodies were stalling and a chorus of fetal heart tones sang out in the room like horses galloping.

Today, though, I was done with all of it.

When Dustin finally woke up, I lay there for a while without saying anything, waiting for the next *ow-ow-ow*.

"Is this it?" he asked me.

My mom came over. "Stuff's...happening," I told her. She got excited; I told her not to. She ignored me. I covered my face with my hands. I flashed back to me walking in on her in the bathroom in 1995 and asking her for a maxi-pad. She had tried to give me a tampon. I shook my head and ran out.

The three of us went for a walk to get things moving. *I should be walking* was all I could think. I drank half an iced coffee and stopped and bent all the way over on street corners. We made it to a park that was just filling up with small children and their mothers, who eyed me suspiciously; I was about to be one of them. I side-eyed them back and then muffled my shouts into Dustin's shirtsleeve. I was improvising escapes from this new pain. I kneaded the flesh of his arms, pulled on his belt loops, yanked at all of his pockets, grabbed him by the hips, then sipped iced coffee and trudged forward in the sun. The pain was now a much sharper, sustained toe-stubbing, like your body being twisted and wrung out from the inside. But temporary! You just had to ride it out. It was almost fun at this point—a personal challenge. "You're going to stub your toe very, very hard every ten minutes for the next few hours, but then you'll have a baby!" That seemed okay—doable.

"Annnnd here we go!" I'd say, then shove my iced coffee into my mom's hands and slam my head into Dustin. I did my breathing, dutifully, skillfully, and I moved around rhythmically, like a belly dancer or a mentally disturbed person. Then the contraction would end and I'd float out above my body and marvel that this was really happening. I'd take back my iced coffee, laugh a little embarrassed laugh, like, *Whew, how 'bout that?* Then as soon as I caught my breath and shook off the pain, I would get yanked back in, like a gust of wind through a subway tunnel, and reconvene with the bodily me, who was having her organs tightened with a belt made of barbed wire.

Knowing this was "normal" was the only thing keeping me from screaming, from calling an ambulance, from preparing for death. I was doing battle, or having battle be done unto me, every seven minutes now.

Back at the apartment, we moved from room to room. I ate piece after piece of watermelon, buried my face in pillows, leaned over tables and countertops, carried my big purple yoga ball around the house and rolled all over it. I thought about how this was almost pornographic, my ass in the air, me moaning.

I wore my blue-and-white-striped maternity dress, crew socks, and purple Crocs.

I labored in a dress? I labored in a dress.

At some point, the contractions were three minutes apart. Then five. Then three. It was now six p.m. Dustin phoned the on-call OB and then hung up and said he'd call a car. That's when the contractions stopped.

I stood up from being bent over the butcher block and looked at the timer on my phone, bereft. Ten minutes. Then seven. Then ten. Then twelve. Then fifteen. I panicked. We walked. Ten minutes. Twelve minutes. Twenty minutes! Soon it was late. I argued with Dustin over how long a normal labor was, listing friends whose labors were six hours or eight hours. "That's not normal!" he said. "Yes, it is!" I snapped back. I searched frantically for a worksheet from my yoga teacher about average early-labor durations and couldn't find it. I grabbed my phone and Googled it, which was the way I always tried to win an argument. I spent whole hours wishing my mom would go home and go to sleep, but I was unable to communicate this. She did, finally, and I felt such gratitude. Like maybe now it would work. Maybe she was a psychic block.

We tried to sleep. We slept in intervals of twelve minutes, then fifteen, then twenty, then seven. All along, the worst pain; rocking, cringing, shouting, kneading pain.

By midnight I was in tears and cursing the piece of paper we had hanging on the fridge that told us when we could take this whole labor thing seriously: *3-1-1*. That was the code, drilled into us by the doctor. We could come in when the contractions were three minutes apart, lasted one minute each, and continued in this pattern for one hour.

"Maybe," I whimpered, "this is just how labor is for me. Maybe I'm close. Maybe my contractions will never get closer together. That happened to someone on BabyCenter!" I wanted to be monitored, to make sure the baby was okay. I was still feeling him kick, but who knew? We couldn't see in there, couldn't access his chamber. This was what I hated most about pregnancy and what I wanted over with more than anything: the opacity. I wanted him out where I could see him. But before that, I had to be made to suffer. Before that, this.

When Dustin called the doctor, seeming so grown up in the next room, I got a contraction and made sure to moan extra-loud for effect. Everyone told us the doctors gauge your labor sounds for signs of progress. Dustin paced and reasoned with her and then hung up and came back to me. The on-call doctor had told him that if a patient has been in labor for a long time but her contractions aren't getting closer together, she "lets" them come in at the twenty-four-hour mark to check in and get monitored for a bit. Dustin gave this information to me gently, without the despair I thought the situation called for. He became, then, the enemy too.

"No," I said, crumbling. I needed a fix. I felt unheard, misunderstood. The twenty-four-hour mark of my labor would be at six the next morning, eight hours from now. I was sure I wouldn't make it that long. I'd never make it.

I don't know how I endured the next eight hours, but it mostly involved making deals with myself. *Keep going until two a.m., and then you can reassess. Three a.m. Six.*

And all along—pain, pain, pain. The grooves of it were beginning to feel familiar, well worn. Sore.

Dustin gathering our stuff and calling a car gave me a second wind. It was eight a.m., twenty-six hours in. I felt like a kid about to go on a huge trip. I tried not to grin, feeling the bigness of the situation as I lived it; I was setting off to a terrible fate.

Then I lay screaming on the bed as Dustin popped in, held up different objects, and asked if he should bring them. He picked up the yoga ball and I shook my head no. I was decisive, certain. *No, no, no.* I wanted to show up unarmed. I wanted to be taken care of. There would be no more bouncing.

I hadn't imagined my mom with us for any of this, but there she was and I wasn't going to ask her to leave. She was quiet, like a ghost—a nice ghost, hovering but unobtrusive. When she came over at seven or eight in the morning, she said she'd had a dream we went to the hospital without her. I took that to mean I shouldn't ask her to meet us there later. I said nothing.

It's not that my mom's being there bothered me; it was more that I was constantly evaluating whether her being there bothered me.

We opened the door and I felt like Miss America as I walked out onto the dais of my front stoop. The driver didn't flinch when he saw me. I watched for it. The three of us slid into the backseat, Dustin in the middle. He patted my knee and leaned forward to the cabbie. "She's in labor," he said with comic nonchalance. "You might hear some noises but she's not going to have the baby in the car or anything."

I gripped the handle above the car window, the one that must have been invented for women in labor. I got three contractions during our forty-minute trip to the hospital through rush-hour traffic. I handled them silently, like a professional. We careened across Houston Street, went up the West Side Highway. The wind blew into my face through the open window, saving me. I closed my eyes and breathed it in. It was as if I were on my way to the first day of school.

The problem with walking through the lobby of the hospital and riding up the elevators is that everyone at the hospital is having his or her own moment. This is not the story of you in labor, walking through the hospital. No one is even looking at you. People are dying, or visiting the dying, or coming in for surgery, or leaving after it. People are here to visit babies or ex-wives, to get skin grafts. There is no dramatic music playing as you glide through security. *I'm having a baby!* you want to announce, as if your body doesn't, but no one looks at you.

As we were about to burst through the doors of Labor and Delivery—and there is no other way to enter Labor and Delivery but by bursting—my mom stopped us. "Wait, wait, guys!" she shouted, laughing. "I'm sorry, but let me take your picture." Only one person can accompany the woman in labor into triage, so my mom was about to go back down in the elevator.

In the picture, I'm swollen and huge and have this teenage look, like I'm trying not to roll my eyes.

Just then I had a contraction, a convenient rebuke to anyone who doubted me, my right to be here. "Are you in
labor?" the woman at the first desk asked sweetly. I nodded
my head yes but it was buried in my arms, my forehead resting on the cool laminate counter. There were other people,
people not in labor, looking at me. I didn't have much time
to think about them, which was possibly a first in my life, to
be in such pain that I didn't care anymore what other people
thought of me.

We were called into a big room with a bunch of beds
and curtains. It had been under construction, and there were
ladders and fresh paint, and I worried about the paint fumes
affecting the baby. I was told to go into the exam room
alone. Someone told me to change into a hospital gown and
put my clothes in a bag. The thought of doing this by myself was ridiculous, like they had just left me with an Allen
wrench and told me to assemble my hospital bed, but I did
it anyway, inching my red cotton underwear off in slow motion, gingerly stepping out of one leg and then shaking it off
my other ankle. I stared down at it, overwhelmed and steeling myself for the journey of bending over to pick it up. I
kicked it away from the bed, a stalling tactic. *Uhhhh.* Standing there naked, I puzzled over what I eventually figured out
was a stretchy, crop-top-like thing I had to put over my belly
to hold the monitors in place.

Finally—a monitor. It would show my heart rate and

blood pressure, the baby's heart rate, and my contractions. Being tethered to a machine like this had been presented in childbirth class as a nuisance, but once the nurse came back in and hooked it up, I found the whole thing hugely reassuring, concrete evidence of my subjective experience: *This is happening but you're fine, the baby's fine.* The machine was behind me a bit, over my left shoulder, and I lay in the bed and gazed up at it reverently, craning my neck to see the numbers, flashing in digital green. At this point I didn't believe, really, that either of us, me or the baby, would make it out alive, but the numbers argued otherwise. As long as I kept watching them, I felt like we would be okay.

I told the nurses again and again about my pregnancy, which had been totally uncomplicated—perfect, even. I had been in labor for twenty-eight hours. No one cared. No one gave me a medal or batted an eye. They just nodded and wrote it all down in my chart.

I wished for a way to communicate pain more precisely than on a scale of one to ten. This was the worst pain I'd ever felt, but I had never had my arm cut off. That was what I always imagined to be the worst pain: having a limb chopped off. I saved ten for that, out of respect. I wanted to keep nine for the moment the baby tore his way out of my vagina. That left eight. I wanted to seem brave, so at first I said seven, but then, worried they wouldn't understand the urgency of the situation, I came back with eight.

I tried to communicate in a gesture that I didn't agree with their method, with these yellow emoticons, with the Spanish above it. DOLOR. I stared at this sign, waiting for some answer to come from it. MUY DOLOROSO.

Eventually Dustin came in and held my arm. He felt betrayed, I sensed, that he'd been left out there so long. They asked if it was okay with me if two residents checked me. This was what they called it. They wanted to "check you." *You* means your cervix. *You* are your cervix. *Check* means stick a hand inside of *you*—your vagina—to measure how dilated your cervix is. They do this with their fingertips, because that was where we were at with science in 2014: fingertips were used as a unit of measurement.

"You're a three" meant your cervix was dilated three fingertips. You got checked, typically, at your last few OB appointments. *I* had been found to be closed. Or "soft and closed" or "high and tight." "Low and soft and closed."

After the first resident checked me, he pulled out his hand and it was covered in goo and blood, and as he walked over to the trash to throw away the glove, he kept his two fingers in the fingering position. Maybe I was projecting, but he seemed a little grossed out. I hated him for this, and still do, this resident with a goatee who pretended to be chipper. I'd never had a male ob-gyn before and I would like never to again.

Next came the second resident, who seemed superior to

the first in rank if not humanity. She went in and did something horrible to me in a way I won't ever forget. She stuck her index and middle fingers up there and rammed them around every which way, like she was trying to tear a hole in me. I trusted, with some hesitation, that this was the proper procedure. Someone held my thighs open in goddess pose, feet touching, while I thrashed. I wanted to show up with painted signs and picket about the way this woman was handling my vagina. "Oh my God!" I yelled. She pulled her hand out, satisfied. "You're going to have some spotting," she said, snapping her glove, at least in my memory of her.

If I regret anything about the way I labored, it's the fact that I let two people fish around in my vagina for the sake of their own education. And then worried they weren't pleased with me because I was a "three." I had been in labor for thirty hours. Fuck the world, fuck humanity, fuck God. I looked up at Dustin, scared.

"They want to kick me out," I said.

"Yep," he said.

I have failed them, I'm a fool, the person who shows up at the hospital too early, I thought. The medical professionals came back, sighing. I saw my OB through a crack in the curtain, standing in the hallway chatting with the nurses. She was wearing a dress and heels and glasses, holding a bunch of manila folders, having it all. I hated her for living her business-attire life while I was enduring this.

The resident who'd manually torn open my cervix came back and announced, "Dr. R. had you scheduled to be induced today at four p.m." Dustin perked up at this.

"Oh, really!" he said, sarcastic. "How wonderful of her to let us know!" Normally I would have walked away and pretended I didn't know him, but under the circumstances this was not an option.

The medical staff laughed uncomfortably and shrugged as if to say, *Sorry, this is how it works.* I wanted to be mad but what could I have done? Refused to be induced? (I wrote that as a joke, and yet even now, there is a part of me that is sure that someone made of sterner stuff would have done just that.)

The kindest of the nurses, tall and cheerful and middle-aged, came over to my bedside and spoke soothingly, like a conspirator. "Hey, have you eaten anything? Once you are admitted you can't eat or drink anything, so you might want to go eat lunch then come back!" News to me. I imagined myself at an Indian buffet, crashing face-first into it and then tearing it down with the force of my rage at being born female. Instead I was grateful for the advice and nodded obediently. "Okay, I think we will do that!"

It took what felt like ten years to get dressed again. As Dustin and I were on our way out, the nurse tapped me on the shoulder and, laughing, told me to have a glass of wine and caviar. Then Dustin and I ventured blinking back out into the day that, inexplicably, had been going on without us.

Not five feet out the door, we started our well-worn "What do you want to eat?" routine. It was considerably higher stakes than most days. I didn't want to walk far, but I didn't want to be still either. I wanted not to exist. Men in suits were out on their lunch breaks. We passed by a deli, which looked like the only option. Everything seemed awful. I asked for a plain bagel with cream cheese. I urged Dustin to eat too. He ordered some kind of sandwich but never touched it. On the corner of Fifty-Eighth Street and Amsterdam—a contraction. I leaned against the brick wall and then dropped to my knees. We crossed the street to the hospital and walked up some stairs, and a security guard told me that once we went through the doors I could get a wheelchair. I didn't want a wheelchair, though. I wanted to be able to walk away from my pain.

"Back so soon?" said the nurse from before, and I felt like I had failed her. I hadn't walked enough. I hadn't eaten caviar.

Eventually we got checked in to a birthing room. My new nurse was named Kathleen and she was youngish and sweet and pregnant too. She asked me a series of questions, reading from a clipboard. "Are you in an abusive relationship?"

Only with myself, I thought. Kathleen was proud, it seemed, of my uncomplicated pregnancy. Or I was the proud one, ticking things off: No, no, no. Either way, there was pride in the room. There was a feeling, finally, that I was a good one.

Kathleen said she was going to start my IV. I asked her if I could get a hep-lock, which is like an IV but instead of being attached to bags and machines, it's just a little tube stuck in a vein in your hand, taped down, ready for medication. She said that if I wanted an epidural I'd need an IV. I told her that I didn't think I wanted one. She was taken aback. I was taken aback that she was taken aback. "Okay," Kathleen said, forbearing, but if I *did* want an epidural, I'd need an entire bag of saline first, which would take about forty-five minutes to run. Something about this forty-five minutes, of all things, unnerved me. In some deep corner of my brain, I realized, I'd been soothing myself with the possibility of instant relief. Not that I would take it, but knowing I had an out if I needed one was what made the pain endurable. I was *choosing* it.

Nurse Kathleen said she had to ask if I could have a hep-lock. She seemed a little put out by this.

"Okay," I said in a small voice. "Can you ask?" She nodded and left.

So this is why people get doulas, I thought. I was going to have to be my own doula, to keep asserting my right to an unmedicated childbirth. I chanted the particulars of our

"Birth Priorities" Google Doc in my head to steel myself. *Hep-lock. Intermittent monitoring. Do not receive pain medication unless absolutely necessary.*

Just then a particularly strong contraction came over me. Doubled over in pain, I found myself studying the cabinets of medical supplies. I saw that one had been labeled, with a label maker, AMNIOTIC HOOKS. I could see stacks of what looked like big plastic knitting needles wrapped in cellophane. Part of me wanted to take a picture, but when you're in labor you don't really keep your purse on you.

They were going to break my water with a knitting needle. I knew it was coming for me. They'd warned me in triage; the nurses said it would be the first step the doctor would take to get labor progressing. This had seemed like a good idea in the abstract but now the thought of lying back and having someone stick one of these things inside of me made me queasy and furious. To have the invasion—the violation—along with the pain was too much. I stared at the white hospital sheets, then the cabinet. I felt my legs go weak. As soon as Nurse Kathleen came back into the room with the hep-lock, I stood up and, almost without thinking, said, "Actually, I want the epidural."

Dustin looked at me. "Are you sure?" he asked in his supportive-but-firm birth-partner voice. "This isn't what we talked about." He put his hand on mine, stared right into my eyes. "This isn't what you wanted."

"None of this is what I wanted!" I snapped at him. I had wanted to do it without any help, yes. I had drunk the Kool-Aid. I had wanted a "natural labor and birth" for reasons that, now that I was actually living through natural labor, I no longer related to. A different person had set this goal, someone who'd been attached to the idea of "being present" and "getting the full experience" before she'd known what the experience would be like. Someone who, when she made her precious little plan, was not imagining this. Wasn't it really just the overachiever in me, my stubborn pride, wanting to prove to everybody—especially myself—that I could do it? I knew, also, that I was deeply afraid of so much and that I had imagined if I felt everything—every terrible sensation—then I might earn some better outcome. I'd imagined that if I could withstand all the pain, take it on and ride it out, "make friends" with it, observe it at a remove, I would be rewarded somehow. Bragging rights? Bodily transcendence? Lifelong confidence? I wasn't exactly sure, but other women had promised me all of that, whether they'd intended to or not. Now my stubborn perfectionism receded with each contraction. The pain eclipsed whatever bullshit messages I had internalized. I didn't care anymore.

People talked about the necessity of "riding the waves" of contractions, submitting to the pain and letting it wash over you. *Try to look into the pain and see what it looks like... imagine you're seeing the feeling under a magnifying glass and slowly studying the edges of the pain... does the feeling have any colors or textures?* I could see the wisdom of this advice. I believed in it, but I couldn't do it. I couldn't keep fighting against my instincts—my personality, perhaps, or something more elemental—which shrank from pain and difficulty. I was washed up, exhausted, desperate for an end. This had gone on too long. What could be more "natural" than the end? I was a dehydrated corpse out in the middle of the ocean, bloated with salt water. Hook me up to a buoy, man. Helicopter me out.

Fuck this shit, I thought. *Bring on the cascading interventions.* And they came.

Soon the epidural crew wheeled on in with their cartoon shower caps and sneakers and fancy watches and black-framed glasses, their well-toned physiques—anesthesiologists, it turns out, are the only doctors who look like TV doctors. The energy in the room immediately shifted. Before they came in, I was a decrepit sea log being beaten upon by the waves, my mother, fiancé, and nurse waving from the shore, feeling helpless and horrified, bearing witness. After the team came in, my body was a thing to be beaten, a war to be won.

The very word *epidural* filled me—and still fills me—with panic. Obviously, the epidural is a routine thing, but it's also, as they were legally required to remind me, a surgical procedure. Hence the shower caps. I was given one, too, in all my pain. No one made sure I tucked my hair in perfectly, which I thought about a lot as they started in on me. Would a hair fall into my spinal column? They talked quickly, all of them drunk on power, slightly manic. I felt like I was being inducted into something (I was), like maybe I was brave for choosing this, for choosing relief, for doing what I wanted despite being afraid of it. Like: *Here we go.*

The nurse has you squeeze a pillow to your very pregnant belly and hunch your back so that your upper body forms a C. She has your birth partner sit on a little chair in front of you, at eye level. You focus on him. Never have I hunched and focused so hard. I could have hunched that baby right out. The doctors paint that sterilizing iodine all over you and feel for your spine, and I worried that I was too fat for them to find my vertebrae and fought the urge to ask them if they were absolutely sure they had put the target in the right place. They used permanent ink to mark where to stab me— I saw the spot a few days later, when I was up and walking. There was also a bruise. A bruise on your spine! There is something viscerally disturbing about all of this, isn't there? Can you feel the twinge in your spine? Are you about to pass out? (Yeah, me too.)

So they stick a big needle into your back and you jump and are sure you have just paralyzed yourself. The first needle is to numb your skin, and then a bigger hollow needle goes in; this one has a tiny tube that gets threaded into the space next to your spinal cord. It seems like you shouldn't feel it, but you totally feel it. You feel like someone is stapling your back, but deep inside you. Stay still, though, or you'll be paralyzed.

I bored my eyes into Dustin and broke into a fear sweat. I was in some kind of war. Wasn't I? This was my moment, my big test, and I was rising to the occasion. I would save the world. Except I wasn't saving the world. I was doing the most banal thing in the world. I was giving fucking birth.

The doctor spoke to me over my shoulder. "Okay, I am going to put in the medicine now. You might feel a shock go through your legs, almost like you put your finger in the electric socket."

What? "Okay." I nodded. Then my legs, hanging off the side of the hospital bed, shot up into the air on either side of Dustin. And, yes, an electric shock shot through me. It was horrible. "Wow, you weren't kidding." They taped me up and told me to lie down on my back. Like, just lie down right on top of the tube that is snaking up next to your spine and don't even think about it. This was really hard at first, as anything spine-related, in my book, should be.

My legs, by this point, were just big meat sticks attached to my body. It's as if your foot has fallen asleep, but it's the entire lower region of your body. Your subconscious is screaming out that something is terribly wrong: *I can't feel my legs!*

I tried to move them to make sure I still could, to shake them back into being. It didn't work. I dragged my huge, lumpen legs across the crinkly paper of the hospital bed, and they fell into place. I looked at the monitor. I was having wild contractions, apparently. The little squiggly line on the machine ratcheted up and up and up and I didn't feel a thing. Disembodiment complete, I asked for my iPhone.

Dustin dug it out of the bag we'd packed and off I went, texting friends in a big group I'd assembled for the occasion. Everyone sent strings of manic emojis when I first wrote to say I was in labor, but when I checked in again, Halle wrote back to say she was so scared I hadn't updated them since the day before. I told them it was hell, then asked my mom to take a picture of the urine bag that was hanging off the side of my hospital bed so I could text it to them. Proof of life. Proof I had maintained my sense of humor and was therefore going to be okay.

Soon my OB came in to break my water. The hook! I spread my legs, or let them be spread, for what felt like the millionth time that day, in the way they preferred—bottoms of your feet touching, knees flopped open, legs in a diamond shape.

I don't remember any great amniotic balloon pop, but I remember the warmth spreading all over and under me.

Like sitting in a bowl of chicken soup. It was beyond pee. And it kept happening, too, for hours. I'd shift, and more soup. It did make me feel plentiful. I contained multitudes. Of amniotic fluid. And then the contractions really started going, up off the charts. The line on the monitor formed a series of waves with valleys and peaks of varying steepness. Now they would peak and then plateau, staying high up, resting there in the pain that I knew was happening but didn't feel.

Until I did. *Until I did.*

Here was the soul-crushing pain again, like a monster who had mercifully passed me by only to catch my scent and come thrashing back down the hallway to find me hiding in some closet. I gripped the bars of my hospital bed as if I could pull myself away from it. I was still numb everywhere—except, inconveniently, the right side of my uterus—so I couldn't move. I had gone through the personal nightmare of getting the epidural, I had mentally exited the battle of contractions, and yet here they were, chasing me down. It was like going through the pain of breaking up with someone and just when you thought you were free, he shows up at your house and, I don't know, throws knives at your uterus?

I screamed in the hospital bed, writhing as much as my numb-meat body would writhe. The winning anesthesiologists came back—an Asian woman I wanted to be friends with entered the room clapping her hands and declaring that they would get me the pain coverage I *deserved.* I perked up at this. Finally someone was concerned with justice. I nodded yes and yes and yes. It was a feminist act, the pursuit of my pain coverage. *Top me off, y'all.* And they did. They topped me off. Then again. And again. And again. I was afloat on a pool of medication, nerve-blocking lidocaine and Tylenol and Sudafed and saline.

And still the pain "broke through." The rest of me just got number. Numb except for about five square inches, where it felt like some demon (male, surely) was chopping at me from the inside with a pickax. My standard writhing and moaning escalated into actual screams. Something about being stuck in the bed, unable to move, and assaulted by terrible pain after I thought pain was behind me made me want to die, sincerely. I peered through my hair and the handles of the hospital bed to see my various attendants standing there, staring at me impassively. My heart rate was sky-high; psychologically, I was in extremis. "I want to die!" I yelled to them repeatedly, but no one did anything. It was like some sort of nightmare, where you scream but no one hears you.

"This is normal, baby," Dustin said, bending over the bed. He was trying to soothe me, to reassure me I would be okay. I gripped his hand desperately.

"No, it isn't," I said, looking at him, pleading with him to hear what I was saying.

"Yes, it is," he said, his face next to mine. Traitor.

"It's not okay," I hissed. "I want to die. I want to die." I rolled around in the bed feeling like a child. His brave face only made me feel crazier. I felt trapped in the subjective experience of my body, wishing I could wave a magic wand and give them my pain, just for a second, so they would take me seriously. I felt like I was drowning and everyone was watching from a few feet away, doing nothing. Just waiting for me to calm down.

Then my OB came in and announced that she wanted to "check" me. My obstetrician was a five-foot-tall black woman who wore her hair parted down the middle and pulled back in a ponytail. She was no-nonsense, cerebral, had a nervous, matter-of-fact patter that always made things like breast exams less awkward.

When another contraction started she gave me a little talk about how sometimes people just had a "blind spot" when it came to pain relief and no amount of epidural would cover it, and her professionalism began to feel like cruel apathy. I interrupted her multiple times to scream, but she just kept talking over me, not missing a beat. She was used to the likes of me, inured to the screaming. She started to check me, and when she instructed me, midcontraction, to "relax or I can't do it," I thought about her wedding announcement, which I'd found upon Googling her back in the day. It said she'd found love for the first time at forty-three. I was always charmed by this, always half tempted to ask her about it, but now I just considered it confirmation that she had never been in labor and therefore had no idea what was happening to my body and my mind. I shrank back into myself. I was being pummeled. I felt like a madwoman, existentially alone, climbing the walls. Then came a strange, unwelcome solidarity with all women. The certainty that we were damned.

"Just knock me out!" I cried to the doctor as my latest contraction tapered off. I was joking, but the joke was that I said it out loud. I had never asked for something more sincerely.

"We're not going to do that." The doctor chuckled, exchanging glances with the nurse. I peered out at her from behind my pain, through a crack in the bed rails. The alarm on my heart-rate monitor started going off, making the room sound like the inside of my head, and a new troop of shower-capped people came running in, all very concerned about my heart when they should have been concerned about my pain.

Wanting to try to go without the epidural was one thing; getting it and having it fail was quite another. It was unjust. It was traumatic. *My stupid body,* I thought. *My awful gender. The limitations of medicine. Of sex. Of humanity. Fuck it all. I don't deserve this.* And I meant that. I still mean it. Of course, outwardly I just nodded, scrunched up my entire being, and felt a little glimmer of hope. Then fear. Then hope. Then pain, pain, pain.

My family still sat beside me but I was alone, inescapably tethered to my body.

I did not want to experience another epidural, but in the deranged game show of this childbirth, that was the prize behind the curtain. The left side of my body was heavy and barely there. All of the extra epidural was definitely pooling in that area. We rocked my body back and forth—I say "we" because there is no way I could have turned myself—hoping that the epidural would drip, would run over to the right. This did not feel very scientific. And it did not work.

Soon another doctor came in and tried to put me at ease. An old pro, I had been pulled into a seated position and was hunched over my hospital pillow, staring at Dustin again. Once again, getting the epidural filled me with visceral horror, but within minutes my pain was gone.

My OB came back in so she could check me properly. She groped and prodded and shoved unnamed objects around inside of me, trying to find the baby's head.

Oh yes, the baby. He was in there through all of this. The thought of that now seems bizarre. At the time it was so much about me, my body, my pain. Part of me—most of me—didn't believe I'd ever see him. Certainly not alive.

Soon, Dr. R. stood up from her perch beside my (at this

point ironically named) birth canal and folded her hands together on top of her clipboard. (Did she have a clipboard? Everyone seemed to. Everyone seemed to have the answers to the problem of me written on their clipboards, just out of my reach.) She told me, in a tone I imagined she usually reserved for informing family members that their loved one was dying, that my cervix hadn't moved. I was still a three or a four or a five, I don't remember. It didn't matter. Whatever I was, it wasn't enough. Worse yet, the baby's head was "floating." This was not good. My child was bobbing within me, treading water. He did not want to make the trip. Could I blame him?

"He could be stuck," she said. "There's no way to know for sure, but if his head is lodged in your pelvis, it could be pulling on your ligaments and causing breakthrough pain." As she spoke, I felt it again, the pain sneaking up, the way you hear keys in the door before someone walks in.

"Epidurals cover pain, not pressure," she told me, explaining that the baby's head was possibly—just a conjecture, of course—slamming into the right wall of my uterus and tugging at my ligaments, yanking the entire side of my body up and down with the contractions. There was nothing they could do about that, really. What I felt, though, was pain, unmistakably. The worst pain I'd ever felt. Possibly the pain of my ligaments being torn from the bones of my pelvis? Sure.

Dr. R. had raised the possibility of this happening at one of my last prenatal checkups as she'd eyed Dustin, who at six two is more than a foot taller than me. "Your genes might be mismatched," she'd said matter-of-factly, meaning that it might be a case of a Dustin-size baby trying to get through a me-size pelvis. "What size shoe do you wear?" she asked me, then clucked and shook her head when I said five. "Supposedly the size of your pelvis correlates with your feet," she said. "It's an old midwives' thing." I'd been charmed by this information that afternoon, but thinking of it now made me furious. *They can measure the thickness of my baby's neural tube eleven weeks after he was conceived, but they can't tell me if his head will fit through my pelvis? What is science even for?*

This was when they all started looking at the clock, tapping their watches. It was just like all the natural-birth advocates warned it would be: Other people were impatient with my suffering. Except now that I was in it, I felt like tapping my watch too. My normally fast-talking OB crossed her arms and began dragging out her syllables. "Wellllll, at a cerrrrtain point we have to take a step back and aaask ourselves..."

She gave me two options. One was starting Pitocin, a medication that induces labor but also strengthens contractions. If my contractions were stronger, hey, maybe my baby, who had been squeezed for days now, would get squeezed on down through my vagina. The other option was that I could get, you know, the thing. The thing women in labor are supposed to avoid at all costs. The failure. The intervention to end all interventions: the C-section. It was totally up to me.

At this point, I desperately wanted someone to strap me down and put me out of my misery, but I am also a stubborn bitch who did not want to fail at birth. I did not want to fail to *give* birth. "So, what if you induce me," I said from behind a wall of pain, "and it doesn't work? Which it probably won't, if his head is stuck?"

"Well, I wouldn't say *probably*. My guess is he is stuck, but there is no way to know. But yes, you could still end up with a C-section. I can't really say either way."

"Okay," I said. "So we should do the Pitocin. Right?"

"I can't tell you what to do," she said. "It's not my body." If only it were. "If we do the Pitocin, though..." And she continued moving her mouth and uttering sounds as I felt my contractions breaking through the second epidural.

"...and that would mean possibly hours more of contractions, then the whole pushing stage..."

The thought of staying awake twelve more hours and then actively pushing was unfathomable. I looked at Dustin. "What do you think?" I asked him, begged him to tell me. He was at a loss too.

"Whatever you want to do. It's your body." I hated this. Stop reminding me. I had to endure the physical agony; at the very least, someone else should have to do the mental arithmetic.

I wanted the C-section so badly. I wanted it like you want a glass of water at a stranger's house but feel like you should demur for some reason. I wanted it the way you want someone to stick a finger in your butt during sex but would never ask for it. I was thinking like a woman. I was in the most essentially oppressed, essentially female situation I've ever been in and I was mentally oppressing myself on top of it.

"I should do the Pitocin, right?" I looked around at everyone in a panic. I wanted to know everyone's honest opinion. I wanted to know what they would think of me either way. Would I make a decision and would they all judge me internally? Would they all think, *Well, that was definitely the wrong call, but okay!*

"We can't tell you," they kept saying. My doctor shrugged behind her clipboard, clearly growing impatient. I stared at her and said nothing. She didn't offer to give me time. She just kept saying it wasn't an emergency. And yet. And yet the clock was ticking anyway. It was an emergency of capitalism, of everyone being sick of my shit. Lucky for them I was sick of my shit too. Utterly. I wanted the C-section. "But the recovery!" I said out loud. I knew you were supposed to think about this, be haunted by this; it was supposed to keep you from "giving in," but damn if I could think beyond the pain of the now.

Another chorus of "It's up to you." I had a diaper full of ice on my head to combat a mild fever that had come on a few hours earlier and wouldn't go away, and it kept slipping off. Everyone stared at me, waiting. I stared at the ceiling and tried to concentrate, thinking, *If only I didn't have to make this life-or-death decision with a diaper on my face.*

I imagined dying during the surgery. Bleeding out or something similarly horrible. What if they went to cut me open and accidentally sliced the baby? This happens. Or has happened, which for the purposes of my monkey mind were one and the same.

It would be my responsibility. *She died during her C-section. Well, she chose it, so...* I would become an argument for not going into the hospital before 3-1-1. A case discussed in birth classes everywhere. Ina May Gaskin would write about me in the updated editions of all her books.

But then part of me shifted. I'm not sure which part; some *You don't have time for this shit* part. Some *Do what you fucking need and fuck everyone else, fuck what anyone thinks* part. This part of me woke up, and I looked around the room feeling, for what might have been the first time, a near-religious conviction: it was time for this part to be over.

"Okay, give me the C-section."

Everyone nodded, said, "All right!" It was like I had just read out from the playbook at the big game and my team had clapped their hands and gone running. It happened about that quickly too. As soon as I said, "Give me the C-section," I got, for the first time, genuinely excited to meet my baby, as if this whole natural-childbirth thing, long ago thrown out the window, had been a sort of block. The smoke had cleared and we were finally going to do the thing we'd come here to do, people.

Dr. R. told me she would go write my name on the whiteboard, which loomed large in my imagination thanks to television sitcoms, and she must have known it. Then I would be "on the schedule." I got the impression this might not happen for a while, and I would have the opportunity to get used to the idea—that is, freak out about it, Google it on my phone between contractions, make Dustin console me, find out if he thought it was the right decision, apologize ahead of time in case I had just volunteered to go to my death. Was I walking the plank? (I was always walking the plank.)

What felt like thirty seconds later, a team of people scurried into the room. They must have detached wires and tubes from me. I think they placed my bag of pee between my legs. I think they moved me into a portable bed but I don't remember. It was all so fast, this nonemergency.

Only one person could accompany me into the operating room, the nurses announced in the hallway. Who would that be? Dustin quickly raised his hand. "Me." He was so serious; sure. My mom rushed up to me in the bed, put her head next to mine, and said she was so proud of me.

"You're going to have a baby," she said. "You made the right decision," she said. I shrugged, but she was emphatic. I hadn't asked her opinion in the birthing room, but maybe I should have. She cried and kissed me and told me she'd see me soon and I heard someone herding Dustin somewhere to get suited up. They wheeled me along, through double doors, just like you imagine. Everyone was happy, and I got happy too. I was no longer oppressed. I was liberating myself from the tyranny of the body.

It really did feel like that, like man triumphing over man. Or man triumphing over woman. Over nature. What was nature, anyway? Nature was cruel; nature was indifferent to my pain. Nature was catastrophic. Nature needed man to intervene. Science, technology, medicine. This was what was called for. How had I ever thought otherwise?

And then there I was, in the operating room. I couldn't believe how much like an operating room it felt. Cold, bright lights, antiseptic, people scurrying around and chatting with each other. It was like being present at my own death, except once in a while someone would ask me a question.

"You're smiling again," the doctor said to me. "Guess you're feeling more like yourself."

I stared at the ceiling tiles and thought about personality, wondering if the pain had made me more myself or less.

They told me that they were going to move me from my wheeled bed to the table. "Oh, boy," I said. I was a rock from the belly button down. They coached me somehow and I said, "I don't think I can do much!" and the doctor said, "Don't try to help us at all!" and she and another tiny woman heaved me—rolled me, really—over to the operating table. I helped them shuffle my half-corpse to the center. It was a disturbingly narrow table. People had to be able to reach over me and into my body cavity, so I guess it made sense.

They were going to prep me first, and then let in "Dad." Poor, sweet Dad, stuck in the hallway somewhere. Were they putting the scrubs on him, turning him into an archetype? Dad at the Birth of His Son. They said they didn't want Dad to see the prep. They wanted everything all set up and covered up and hidden before he came in. *Must be nice,* I thought, but also: *Why spare him?*

Someone spoke to me from a place I couldn't see. "Sometimes they get squeamish," he said. "Does Dad have any issues with this, Mom?"

Who were these Mom and Dad people they kept talking about? "No," I said, trying to defend his reputation. Then I remembered that he actually was squeamish, or so he had told me.

"Actually, it's hard to say," I said. "We've never done this before." Everyone laughed. Maybe making jokes while splayed out naked would help me dissociate. A woman had an electric razor out and was shaving my pubic hair. I debated asking her if she accepted tips and decided against it.

When had I slipped onto the set of the scary government-hospital scene in *ET*? It was horrific, but I felt at peace, like things were being taken care of finally. This I could endure.

There was a new anesthesiologist, and he introduced his assistant to me. She was Southern, pretty, youngish, and on her first day back from maternity leave. Her baby was four months old, a girl. She missed her, but it was nice to be back. She'd ended up with a C-section too, she told me. "You're going to feel really, really weird stuff, okay?" she said. "I mean, *really, really* weird. It's so weird. But you're going to meet your baby really soon. It's so exciting!" I nodded. She was my new mother. I had to keep it together for her.

Pressure, though. You feel pressure. How is this possible, pressure and not pain? I could feel them tapping my pregnant belly. I told the woman, my new mother, that I felt strange lying on my back. "I know, right?" She laughed. "But it's okay." You weren't supposed to lie flat on your back during pregnancy for fear that the baby would rest on your aorta and compress it, decreasing the blood flow to both of you.

I imagined coming all this way only to have the baby die because I was lying flat on my back on the operating table.

Before Dustin could come in, they hung up a sheet blocking my view of my naked body and bulging belly. My arms were spread wide, the table shaped like a crucifix. The drugs made me shake. I was cheerful and scared and so, so excited all at once. I was running a marathon and would get a baby at the end. My teeth chattered. My arms flopped around on the crucifix table. I asked if this was normal. It was totally normal. They said it was partially hormonal and partially the medication. I kept apologizing. *No, honey, no. This just happens. It's okay.* Shake-shake-shake. I tried to treat my body like a science experiment, to float above it and simply observe. On some level I loved being there, witnessing this horrific scene.

"Okay," the new mother said, "your husband is coming in soon."

"Fiancé," I corrected her. Normally I would have gone with it, with *husband*, but this seemed like official business, like our passports would be checked at the end and they'd look at me and shake their heads. A liar. A liar with a child.

"Oh, okay. Your fiancé will be here soon."

(I hated saying *fiancé* during pregnancy; I felt it conjured obligation.)

A man's voice called out to me from somewhere in the room.

"Boy or girl?"

"Boy!" I said, trembling, grinning. We were shouting to each other like acquaintances in a loud bar.

"What's his name?"

"We don't know yet!" I laughed. We all laughed. People in scrubs and masks shook their heads.

"Gonna wait and meet him, huh? I like that!"

He didn't have a name because so far nothing had felt right. We wanted, or I wanted, a revelation. A name that was traditional, simple, strong, but that all of society had somehow forgotten; a name that we alone had unearthed. I wanted other new parents to kick themselves, wishing they'd thought of it first. I wanted it to be hiding in plain sight.

This never happened.

The anesthesiologist's assistant offered me "something," as in "I can give you something. A sedative." I nodded, shaking. *Yes. Give it to me.* I had been basted like a turkey at this point. Nothing fazed me. Drugs were now my friends.

The curtain was up and my new mom was explaining to me how they would get the baby out. They would not be, as I'd imagined, plopping my uterus onto my stomach and tearing it open like a Christmas present. They would make a three-inch incision at my bikini line. (I had never worn a bikini in my life, and I certainly never will now. It's hard to remember what was there before.)

In order for the baby to emerge through this little slit, he would have to be pushed out. He would have to be born.

My doctor gave birth to my baby.

I didn't even particularly like my doctor. I liked her as a character. I liked her from afar. I admired her. I would never have chosen to socialize with her. She made me uncomfortable. Every interaction with her, I was left feeling like *What was that? Why was that so hard?* Somehow, this helped me trust her.

So my doctor, the anesthesiologist's assistant said to me, would be climbing on a chair and leaning all of her weight onto my abdomen and literally pushing my baby out of me. She'd knead him down from the outside. Shove, shove, shove, so that he finally stopped bobbing and was forced out, once and for all. As the anesthesiologist's assistant explained how strange this would feel, they started cutting. They whispered so that I wouldn't hear. What were they whispering? *She's bleeding out, what should we do? I don't know, but look at this gigantic tumor here. Wow, is this woman fat. I mean, I know she's pregnant, but still.*

While I shook and smiled at the anesthesiologist's assistant and strained to decipher the whispering, my stomach flipped with excitement. I was thinking I'd meet him soon, that this might be it. Was he really going to live? What would they find wrong with him that they hadn't seen on ultrasound? Just then someone yelled, "Where's Dad? Did we bring in Dad? Bring in Dad!"

Before I could turn my skull full of chattering teeth to the left, there he was, hovering over me as if in a dream. I'd never been so happy to see him in my life. My love. Everything was better in this room with him in it in a shower cap, looking like dads do in the movies, in shades of hospital teal and baby blue. He had a gown on, too, over his clothes. And a surgical mask. Something about him in this uniform, this signifier of childbirth, helped what was happening seem okay. It was precedented, normal, familiar. I'd seen it on television. This was just our turn. He sat on a stool near my head and held my hand, tangled in IVs. His surgical mask was wet with tears and snot.

Our baby. His baby. I felt that for the first time, then. This baby was ours, yes, but it was also mine and then it was his in ways that our relationship couldn't encapsulate. This baby was each of ours, privately.

My woman, my new mother, told Dustin to get his camera ready. He only had his cell phone—our new camera, bought with this moment in mind, was in the hallway with my actual mother. She told him that he could stand up and look when they were pulling the baby out, that when she said so, he could take a picture.

He got the phone ready and I could tell by his eyes that he was smiling under the surgical mask. He told me later that I was out of it, not myself, but I didn't feel that way at all. I felt tuned in, like the thick fog of bodily horror had finally receded and I was all brain, all soul, at one with the universe and the immensity of the moment.

"Okay!" she said, tapping me. "They're going to start pushing him out! It's going to feel really weird, okay? But that's normal!" She held my right hand, Dustin my left. I tried not to play with her engagement ring. The diamond was huge. Her hands were perfectly manicured. I loved her in that moment, this woman I'll never see again. I wouldn't recognize her even if I did.

They started to tug, and the force of the tugging had my half-dead body swaying like a canoe. I stared straight ahead as if to focus on the task at hand. The task at hand was to not scream, to not use whatever strength I had left to fling myself off the operating table. The task was to endure the most bizarre experience of my life, the feeling, painless, of someone yanking all of your organs out. *I am a vessel only. I am something to be pillaged. A cabinet, a pantry door. I am lying naked on a table in a cold room under bright lights, my arms splayed out to form a T, and a team of people are gathered around my body, peering into it, excavating it.*

The doctor, my doctor, put a knee up on the table for

leverage. I could see her ponytail bobbing above the curtain. She made a little joke, I don't remember what, her voice straining with effort. We laughed nervously.

And then I heard a cry.

This isn't possible, it's an incorrect feeling, if feelings can be described as incorrect, but what I felt above all at that moment was recognition. Hearing his cry was like seeing a familiar face in a crowd. I was lying on my back staring at the ceiling, shaking, tears streaming down my cheeks. His cry, I was surprised to find, sounded like him. He sounded like his own person. Before that moment, all baby cries had sounded the same to me, but his cry was a voice. A self.

I couldn't see him but this fact didn't bother me. I did not pull him out of me and straight to my chest, the way women did in the videos I'd watched while pregnant. No one shouted, *Catch your baby! Reach down, Meaghan, and catch your baby* the way I'd been imagining. He did not crawl up my stomach and latch onto me. Nothing was how I pictured it when I'd pictured "the perfect birth." Although Dustin was, now that I think of it, telling me I was "doing so good."

I was doing so good, in that I wasn't having a panic attack. I was enduring. My baby had lived. I had lived through this. They hoisted the baby up, and Dustin stood up from his stool and took a picture with his iPhone. We were crying and kissing through his snotty surgical mask and the anesthesiologist's assistant squeezed my hand and kept telling me, "Oh, he is really, really cute."

All of the doctors and nurses commented on how big he was. I couldn't see any of it at the time, but in photos he looks big and blue, like a slimy teddy bear in my doctor's hands. The umbilical cord snakes around the blue sterile paper. There is a hole in my body. My doctor is smiling, one hand on my kid's swollen balls and another behind his neck. He's screaming. Why is my doctor in my son's very first photo? I like to look at it, like hearing about a party I didn't go to. ("Are those my boobs"—Dustin and I squinted at the photo for a very long time; we turned the phone this way and that—"or my thighs?" They were my thighs. "Wow," I whispered under my breath.)

I never even saw my placenta, despite all the back-and-forth about whether or not I should get it encapsulated. That I'd even considered this option struck me as ridiculous once it came down to it, as did so many of the ways I had suspended my disbelief around childbirth, imagining that I would instantly become a different person the moment he was born.

Soon I heard a great sucking noise; someone was suctioning liquid out of the baby's lungs or out of my body cavity. We were the same in that way—underwater.

They called Dustin over to watch him get weighed,

measured. The baby looks so alone in the photos, lying by himself on that scale. A minute or two later, there they both were, with me, the baby wrapped in a blanket, subdued in his father's arms. I tipped my head back, my chin up, to get a good look at him. I struggled to lift my arm, to touch his cheek. I put my face to his face. I didn't know what to say, how to touch him. "Hi, baby," I said, still crying. He looked so distinct, so himself, so...*cute.* That hackneyed word was all I could think of when I looked at him. ("I mean, he's objectively cute, right?" I'd say to all the nurses in the following days, forgetting that I was in an oxytocin haze and anything but objective.)

The anesthesiologist's assistant took a photo of the three of us using Dustin's phone, and then the baby and Dustin went somewhere for tests or baths or who knows what while I stayed on the table, immobile, emptier, unraveled. "Are we almost done?" I asked, laughing weakly.

The anesthesiologist's assistant patted my hand. "Yes. Almost there. You're doing great," she said, peering over the curtain. "It won't be long. Looks like they're putting you back together right now."

Sleepless Nights

IN THE BEGINNING there was only me on our green couch and the baby in my arms, on my breast. Dustin paced around the fixed point of us, bringing me food and water, taking the baby from me occasionally so that I could sit back with my breasts exposed and try to catch my breath before he cried again. It was mid-June, summer in New York, but we barely noticed. I was sweating, and bleeding, and covered in dried milk. I felt like I had been camping for a week with no running water, except that on camping trips you get to sleep.

We slept in short bursts. Whether the baby was crying or not, I woke up with a start and rushed over to him to make sure he was alive. Day and night bled into each other, coalescing into one big nightmare. My clothes were indistinguishable from pajamas. A lamp was always on. We were in the middle of what felt like an ongoing emergency. Like someone was playing a practical joke on us. Endure the car crash of childbirth, then, without sleeping, use your broken body to keep your tiny, fragile, precious, heartbreaking, mortal child alive. Rock, sway, bounce, pace, sing, hum—Dustin did anything to keep him from crying but it always came back to me, my swollen breasts, nipples scabbed over, milk dripping everywhere and the baby flailing. My arms were sore from holding him, my shoulders so tense from anxiety they were up to my ears. To stand up and go to the bathroom without searing pain and the feeling of my guts threatening to come pouring out of my C-section incision, I had to lie horizontally on the couch and then gingerly roll off it, like a stuntman rolling over the hood of a taxicab.

As the days accumulated, getting through them got harder. We had been home with the baby only three days and I kept waiting for some sort of plateau, some easing up. Instead, he became more and more precious to me and, with every sleepless night, the world more full of sharp edges. I was injured and sleep-deprived and trying to figure out breastfeeding and trying to reckon with the intensity of love I felt, and its attendant fear. The future stretched out in front of me with menacing blankness. Anything seemed possible. Any horrible thing. *Eighteen years,* I thought, and my breath caught.

I tried to watch TV while I fed the baby, thinking I could

treat this time like a snow day, a sick day gone on forever. I would catch up on every prestige television show I'd always meant to watch. In reality I spent most of my time staring at the wall or down at the baby, chasing away forbidden thoughts (*What have we done?*), and counting the hours until I could take another Percocet.

I recorded all of the baby's and my bodily functions in my iPhone, something concrete to stand against the great unknown: *9 a.m. breastfed, left side, 45 minutes / Diaper pee 10 a.m. / Percocet 10:15 / slept 10:20–11.* My record-keeping never cohered into anything meaningful the way I must have wanted it to, but I referred to it constantly anyway. *So this is what we are doing. This is how we are going to survive.* When the baby cried and Dustin brought him over to me with an expectant look, I would wave my phone in his face. "I just fed him twenty minutes ago!" "Well, he seems hungry now. I don't know what you want me to do." The rage I felt at that moment was like nothing I'd ever experienced. I was strung out, under siege, depleted.

Imagine, this was how everyone came into the world. It seemed so extreme. I tried not to think about what life was like just a week ago. Thinking too much, generally, felt like self-harm. Hold the baby, bounce the baby, feed the baby, blot out the fantasies of boarding an airplane, flying to Paris, sleeping in the bookstore Shakespeare and Company, and never coming back. The biggest problem of all was that I loved the baby so immediately and desperately, I knew I could never actually escape. I was not just trapped in our apartment with my tits out, I was also trapped in love with him. I could never go back to before.

Before, before. How had I coped with difficulty before? I would go for a walk with earphones in, disappear into the city, and come back in a few hours when I felt better. Or I would meet up with my friends and talk about whatever was upsetting me until we had it figured out. A walk was physically impossible now, but my friends were coming over in an hour. I knew this "receiving visitors" was a thing that was supposed to happen during our fun-house sick leave—people come, they bring food, you sit back with your feet up and bask in everyone's baby adoration, not worrying for once that the house is a mess. But the thought of ritual, of social nicety, of looking them in the eyes and trying to hold a conversation at a time like this felt ridiculous, impossible.

"These are your friends," Dustin reminded me. *Come over whenever!* I'd finally written, despite my misgivings. *We're just...here.*

Our little apartment had always been a gathering place for my friends. Dustin and I hosted a standing Sunday dinner party for whoever could make it. Our friends carved pumpkins in our kitchen, dyed Easter eggs, made goofy Christmas ornaments and Valentines, and caught up with one another's lives around our tiny yellow table. Now that Dustin and I were home from the hospital, I was waiting for some of that warmth to rush back in. I'd imagined that I would throw open our door with some new maternal confidence—the matriarch welcoming everyone in with French-press coffee and banana bread that I had somehow baked during early labor—and tell them the riveting story of my son's birth.

Now it was clear this had all been magical thinking, but I figured I should at least take a shower.

I winced as I peeled off my maternity leggings and stepped out of the disposable underwear they'd given me at the hospital. I didn't even know where in my body the blood was coming from anymore, but I wore two giant maxi-pads at once and still sat on a towel on our couch, just in case. It seemed like the doctors could have sucked it all out when they were in my uterus, but I bled for weeks. I tried not to look down as I stepped over the ledge of the bathtub, gripping the towel rack with one hand and the shower curtain with the other. The warm water felt weird on my nipples, which stung from being gnawed on twenty hours a day. The peeling paint and plaster on the ceiling of our shower would occasionally rain down. I could see black specks of mold. All of this disgusted me with a new urgency. I felt unsafe and like a bad mother already.

I knew I was supposed to wash my incision but I was

afraid to touch it. I definitely didn't want to look at it. Just thinking about it made me queasy—in fact, my entire torso was a blur in my mind and I was hoping to keep it that way for a while. Everything felt stacked inside of me haphazardly, my body weak and vulnerable when I was supposed to be nourishing and protecting something even weaker, even more vulnerable. I wanted to be present and strong—I wanted to take it all in stride. I wanted to be worthy of my son.

Instead, I felt like something essential in me was threatening to slip. Maybe it already had. I'd spent four days recovering in the hospital, in a shared room. For reasons of privacy, visitors weren't allowed after ten p.m., so Dustin had to leave me alone every night. The nurses insisted on taking the baby to the nursery the first night so that I could sleep for a few hours, which felt bad and wrong but also like the only option, given that my body was still numb from the waist down and I couldn't keep my eyes open. The next three nights they left him with me, and I stayed up all night sweating with the baby slippery on my naked torso (my neighbor was an Albanian woman who had also had a C-section, and when I heard her tell someone that air-conditioning would make her baby sick, I didn't dare press the issue). I sat up in bed crying quietly to myself while the baby screamed, trying to think of ways I could physically slide out of bed with him in my arms without ripping my stitches open and injuring us both. I watched the clock on the wall and counted down the hours until eight a.m., when Dustin would come back to rescue me.

It was better to be home. I turned off the shower and waddled in slow motion over to our bed to get dressed. I'd never felt so physically limited before and was mentally unprepared for it. Our freezer was full of what the internet called "padsicles"—pads Dustin and I had spent one pregnant afternoon soaking in aloe and witch hazel, ready for me to perch on victoriously after my natural-childbirth experience. I had planned to be in pain for a day or two and then ready to go for long walks in the sun with my baby, enjoying time away from work. I had planned for this part to be "hell," but when I'd imagined it, I imagined us overwhelmed but happy, having maintained our sense of humor. I thought the hell would be logistical, not emotional.

Before I dropped my towel, I looked over my shoulder to make sure Dustin couldn't see me from wherever he was sitting. I grabbed one of his big undershirts and my grubbiest pair of underwear and let the towel fall to the ground.

"Oh, hey, I should look at your incision!" Dustin called from the kitchen. "Make sure it's healing okay." Before he could put down the baby and make it over to me, I quickly turned to look at myself in the mirror. It felt important that I see it first. As soon as I did, I broke into the sobs I had been trying to keep at bay all week. I fell apart.

I'd known it would look bad. I'd expected that, and accepted it. All the websites warned you that you'd look pregnant for weeks. Plus I'd always been frustrated with my body, always wanted to lose ten or twenty pounds, always wore a cardigan over a sleeveless dress to hide my chubby arms, dreaded trying on new jeans, blah-blah. *I hate my body already,* I'd figured. *I'll be fine.*

But this was something else. This was undeniable. Undeniably bad. My entire middle section was covered in purplish-red gashes and looked like it was hanging off my body. It looked like a balloon that had been deflated but was also, somehow, full of wet dough. It looked like a beige balloon full of dough that someone had cut purple gashes in. It bore no resemblance to any version of myself I'd ever seen.

Dustin hugged me to his chest and told me he loved me and this was hard but we would be okay, but instead of relaxing into him like I usually did, I stiffened. "It's probably just the hormones," I said, sniffing. "You know, crashing."

He nodded and knelt under me to survey the damage. The lower part of my stomach, the part between my belly button and my crotch, was like a stuffed envelope or a rounded shingle half hanging off the edge of the roof. I stared at the ceiling, willing the tears to stop coming, as I felt Dustin trying to lift this new appendage out of the way so he could examine my scar. I could see him hunching down, craning his neck to see. I felt sick with shame.

"It looks good!" he said, bounding back up. "It's just a little red. It's healing perfectly."

I nodded, humiliated, and pulled up my sweatpants. The baby started to fuss in his little chair so Dustin ran over to him. I pulled a pillow to my face and screamed into it like a teenager, then bit it while I cried. My body, disappointing though it was, had always at least been familiar. Now I was me, but not. Me, but worse. It seemed so unfair, this on top of everything else.

Not long after, the buzzer went off and soon I heard excited voices coming down the hallway, like a threat. I tried to sit up straight, make sure my shirt was buttoned. "Hi," I called over to them from my place on the couch. Halle and Lindsay and Lindsay's husband, Brian, were all half bent over, taking off their shoes and setting their cute bags down by the door. Lindsay proudly held out a lasagna she'd made us. Halle had brought chips and guac. Everyone seemed so lighthearted and congratulatory, ambassadors from some other planet. "We Googled what you're supposed to bring when you come to visit someone's baby," Halle admitted, and we laughed. "Oh. My. Godddddd. Let me see him."

Everyone settled down around the baby and me in the living room and I sat there fighting the urge to snatch him back as my friends passed him around. They looked so natural holding him, so relaxed. So well rested, in pants that buttoned, underwire bras. Their summer wardrobes. Their *summers*. I thought of summer weeks I'd spent grounded as a kid, how I would sit at my bedroom window and wait for the neighbors to come over and talk to me through the screen. They held up toys, entertained me for a while, asked me what I'd done to get in trouble, but eventually they always left to go play baseball or something and I was stuck there, watching them from behind the screen. That's how it felt sitting on the couch across from people I loved, people who knew me better than almost anyone else. Or had until this week.

"So," somebody said, "how *are* you?"

I tried to move the muscles of my face into a smile. "Oh, um...I'm okay, I think?" I searched their eyes for some kind of feedback. Did they think we had made a huge mistake?

"What's it like being a *mom?*" Lindsay asked me. The word *mom* stung.

"God, I have no fucking idea," I said. Her eyes were full of affection and genuine interest, but I felt like she was mocking me, trying to pin me down or reduce me to something. I felt self-conscious, suddenly, in my sweatpants and milk-stained T-shirt. Lindsay's arms were thin and muscular, her hair dyed recently, perfect blond highlights. She looked at me expectantly, smiling, in her expensive white blouse.

"No, I mean, it's good," I said. "It's crazy. I mean, he's amazing. I don't know. We're tired."

Halle looked at me, searching. "So how's he sleeping?"

"Ha!" I said. "Not good." I shifted on the couch, trying to quickly assess whether she really wanted to know or whether this was another question she figured she was supposed to ask. Would there forever be a gulf between us? Did she worry that from now on, all I would have to talk about was banal shit like how the baby was sleeping or how many diapers he went through in a day? (Like twenty, for the record.) We used to stay up late on Gchat crying with each other over things like whether love really existed and, if it did, whether we were lovable or not. We talked about ambition, about the fear of failure, about our endless self-loathing. We rehashed our childhoods, analyzed our parents' relationships, swore we would want more, try harder, be better. Now here I was, sitting on the couch like a sucker, in hell and unable to be honest with myself or my friends.

They asked me to tell them about the birth and I didn't know where to begin. I normally would have been bursting with the news, ready to make jokes and replay each moment, like we did with everything. For the first time in my life I found I couldn't do it. The whole thing was too fresh and too much; it just came to me in flashes. So instead of a story, I recounted the facts. "It was forty hours, I think, start to finish," and "The first epidural failed, which *sucked*, then I had to get another one. Then the C." They nodded and said it sounded horrible. I felt hollow when I just said, "Yeahhhhh." I hadn't figured out how to tell it so that it made any sense. I was afraid it would just sound sad, needlessly hard. I was afraid I would tell it and then realize something that I wasn't ready to know yet. I didn't feel safe enough to poke at the wound.

"Well, you seem like you are doing great, considering," Lindsay said to me and I felt something in me rise up.

"Oh, I dunno," I said, but I was grinning. This was all I wanted to hear. I wanted us to seem happy to them, as ridiculous as it was, like we were coping well. I didn't want my friends to walk out of our house and back onto the sidewalk and cringe at each other. I didn't want them to lie in bed that night feeling grateful it was me and not them.

When the baby started to fuss, I figured it was my way out. "I think I need to feed him," I said, hoping they would take this as a cue to leave. No such luck. Brian and Dustin stood up, clearing their throats, and went scurrying into the kitchen, asking if anybody wanted some water, as I reluctantly unbuttoned my shirt. One indignity after another, it felt like.

"So," I said, pivoting to gossip, now that it was just us. "What's the latest with Jamie—is she gonna have a baby or what?" Here I was, already wishing my fate on someone else.

"Oh, I don't think so," said Halle. "Not yet, anyway."

"Huh," I said, visibly annoyed. I resented anyone still on

the other side, anyone who could still choose not to do it. "I wonder why," I said without a hint of irony.

"Oh," Halle said, "I think she just doesn't want to ruin her body."

"Ha!" I said and then Halle realized what she'd said.

"I mean, not that you did!"

"No, I did." I felt relieved in a way. The elephant in the room. If I'd ruined my body, I should at least get some credit for it. That was part of what was so absurd about our sitting there, my friends acting cheerful and celebratory while I was sinking further and further into despair.

"I'm sure you didn't ruin your body," Lindsay said in a tone that struck me as egregiously knowing.

"Well..." I said, like, *I wouldn't be so sure about that.* Suddenly I had the urge to affront them with my body the way I'd been affronted by it that morning. "Actually," I said, feeling perverse pleasure, "do you guys wanna see my stretch marks? They are fucking insane." My hopes of making a good impression disappeared as they nodded eagerly, leaning forward in their chairs.

"Oh my, yes," Halle said. It was the same thing she'd said when I used to ask her if she wanted to hear some of the lurid details of bad sex I'd had or if she wanted me to forward her an overly emotional e-mail I'd sent to somebody who had screwed me over. Of course she wanted to see. My friends always wanted to see. I had lost sight of that amid all of this. I unlatched the baby and put him down on the couch and then inched my way toward standing upright.

"Okayyyyy," I said, yanking down my sweatpants and pulling up Dustin's undershirt, leaving my horrible midsection exposed.

"Whew!" Halle said with a sharp intake of breath.

"I know," I said. I fought the urge to apologize. I felt like a woman in one of those postpartum-body-acceptance campaigns. I wasn't sure what reaction I was going for. It was somewhere between asking them to tell me that my ass didn't look fat and showing off a war wound.

"Well..." She trailed off, unable to come up with anything.

"Exactly," I said. All three of us laughed uneasily.

"Okay," Lindsay said, all business as always. "It's not *that* bad. I mean, the stretch marks will fade, right?"

"Yes..." I said. "That's what everyone says, but I'll believe it when I see it."

I pulled up my pants and pulled down my shirt, feeling embarrassed but relieved to have someone else look. I needed witnesses. I needed my reality confirmed. I sat back down and held the baby to me and felt lighter somehow. My body was shorthand, living proof. It stood for everything I couldn't say.

We all sat there, looking at one another, unsure what

came next. "Oh, well!" I said and threw up one hand in a fuck-it gesture.

"Yep," Halle said. "What can you do?"

"Not a damn thing," I said, feeling, for the first time, resigned to my fate. My body would never be the same. My life would never be the same. My relationship with these women would never be the same. I couldn't make sense of it yet, even to myself, but I felt like there was a glimmer of understanding between us. We all sank back into the couch cushions and, looking at one another, we shook our heads as if we were shaking them at the universe. At female biology. At love. At everything that came with it. I held the baby to me, happy to be laughing with my friends, even if it was through a screen.

A Certain Kind of Mammal

WHEN I WAS pregnant, every time someone asked me if I planned to breastfeed, I stammered and avoided eye contact. *Of fucking course, what do you think I am, some kind of monster?* I felt like the person had just asked me if I wanted to be a real writer someday. Obviously I thought about it all the time but I didn't want to jinx it by talking about it. Declaring my intentions felt too vulnerable, too potentially humiliating. The question was not whether I planned to breastfeed the future baby but whether I would physically be able to. What if the time came and the baby didn't latch on or my body didn't produce enough milk? What if my boobs couldn't get it up?

The internet was full of stories about women struggling with just that. It was impressive but scary to read about them turning their lives upside down, willing to try or do anything if it meant they could check off this box. Take herbs, chug water, eat special cookies, go to meetings, buy a scale so they could weigh the baby after every feeding, hire expensive consultants, pump around the clock, give up dairy, give up gluten, get their infants' tongues and gums "clipped" so they could open their mouths wider, spend an entire week in bed naked with their babies.

An outsider might find it easy to dismiss this as ridiculous, especially considering you can walk into any grocery store and buy a canister of formula. But, then, an outsider hasn't lain in bed at night facing the harrowing uncertainty of motherhood, desperate to know she was giving her baby "the best start possible."

Whether or not I *would* breastfeed if my body *could* do it, well, that hardly felt like a question to me, not when everything I'd heard or read promised multiple benefits, from increased immunity to a higher IQ. Every parenting website opened the topic with some variation of "Breastfeeding is best for you and your baby, but it can be hard work." They added the part about hard work just for stubborn overachievers like me, I think. Or for people, also like me, who were desperate for direction and found guilt incredibly motivating. "*Best,* you say? *Hard,* you say?" My dog-eared copy of *The Womanly Art of Breastfeeding* had a section called "How Important Is Breastfeeding, Really?" Answer: "Extremely! There is almost nothing you can do for your child in his whole life that will affect him both emotionally and physically as profoundly as breastfeeding." Anyone with a grown child—anyone who's a person!—probably can't read that without scoffing. But before I had the baby, how did I know that? Everything else in parenting was so equivocal, such a gray area. The message in this book, and so many others like it, was the opposite.

"His nursing relationship with you becomes the foundation of the way he will think of himself and others," the book went on. "One mother pointed out that it's as if bottles fill his stomach, but breastfeeding fills his soul.

"Many bottle-feeding mothers wish they had breastfed, yet very, very few breastfeeding mothers wish they had bottle-fed."

I wish I could say I was offended by or at least suspicious of this messaging at the time, but I was in fact the perfect sucker. *Breast is best.* It was so cut-and-dried, it even rhymed. "It's hard work but worth it!" I so wanted to believe that if I "just" exclusively breastfed my baby on demand for a year of his life, I could stave off all the other damage I might do.

I bought nipple cream, nursing bras, special tank tops, reusable ice packs made for boobs. I spent an afternoon on the phone with my health insurance, then ordered a double electric breast pump through Yummy Mummy, a boutique on the Upper East Side. I wrote down the phone number of a local breastfeeding consultant and put it on the fridge, the way my mom used to write the number for our pediatrician on a sticky note for the babysitter. *Just in case.*

It was such a relief to be told exactly what to do.

I was six weeks into my breastfeeding journey when I decided it was time to go back to work. I was on what the staff at the website I edited called maternity leave, but said leave was unpaid and indefinite; I could go back whenever I was ready. I was ready.

In fact, for weeks I'd been desperate to get out of the house and do something I was good at, but so far breastfeeding had made that impossible. I'd taken a few short, hobbled walks to get a juice or a coffee and cry alone on a park bench, but I'd never been gone for more than thirty minutes, and the baby was always crying when I got back.

But now it was time.

I have to work, I started repeating in my head, trying to drum up a sense of urgency. *Work* would mean sitting in a coffee shop blogging. And while it wasn't *technically* true that I *had* to do it, it *felt* true, which was enough. *Work* sounded like something noble, a good enough reason to escape the tiny baby who was hungry around the clock and dependent on my body to stay alive. An excuse to go sit alone somewhere, a person in the world doing something she was good at. *I have to work, and soon,* I thought, or else I'd get swallowed up.

"I think it's time," I said to Dustin one afternoon. I tried to sound somber, to keep myself from smiling when I said it. "I think I'm ready to try working again."

"Okay," he said, matter-of-fact. "When do you want to try it?"

"Tomorrow?" The coffee shop was just at the end of our block, far enough from our apartment that I couldn't hear the baby cry but close enough that I could be home within minutes if I needed to be. Dustin would watch the baby in the morning, and then we would switch and he would go work too. Finally we would start rebuilding something that more closely resembled a life. "It'll be an experiment," I told him. "You know, an hour or two. Just to ease in."

"An hour or so should be okay," Dustin agreed, though I could tell he was nervous. "That's about how long he goes between feeds, right?"

"Yeah!" I nodded my head vigorously, willing it to be true. "Like an hour and a half lately," I said, but in my head I thought, *Two hours.* "Plus I could always pump?"

I had tried the breast pump a few times, recreationally, but not yet so as to explicitly buy time away with my own milk. The pump looked just like I'd imagined, like something you'd use to masturbate a farm animal. The bulk of the machine was a little yellow box the size of a toaster oven that gasped and sighed with a rhythmic, mechanical sucking noise that was initially disturbing, like it was trying to tell me something but couldn't quite find the language. There were two snaking rubber tubes that ran from the box to the air-horn-looking boob funnels and from there into baby bottles that collected the milk. The horns were where the magic happened, where your tits went. Sucked into the machine, my nipples looked like long, pink taffy, stretched and then milked.

The first time I saw milk stream out of my body and into this contraption, I felt woozy and then oddly turned on. It's not often in life we gain a brand-new secretion. But that was in late pregnancy, and now that the baby was here there was nothing sexy about it. There was nothing sexy about anything, actually. And sticking my ragged nipples into a milk machine in the hour between feedings seemed needlessly punitive.

Unless, that is, it buys you freedom. The next morning I packed my laptop in a bag and set the hideous purple Crocs I'd sworn I would wear only during late pregnancy by the door, then I lay down on the bed with the baby to breastfeed him. I put him on one boob and the breast pump on the other. I tapped my foot, looking from baby to pump to clock and back again, knowing that as soon as he unlatched, the timer would start: an hour and a half and he'd be hungry again. And that was being optimistic. He finally pulled off and I jumped up, practically throwing the baby at Dustin.

I'd pumped about an ounce of breast milk from my right breast, which was about a third of a decent feeding at the time. I frowned at it and stuck it in the fridge, knowing I'd be home soon enough anyway.

"When exactly will you be back?" Dustin asked with a concerned look on his face, instinctively bouncing and jiggling the baby.

"Uh, well, he just ate, so... eleven?" I swung my tote bag over my shoulder and tried not to make eye contact with either of them as I inched toward the door.

"Ten thirty," he said.

"What!" I was a teenager negotiating curfew. "I can't get anything done in an hour..." My voice cracked and my eyes filled up with tears as I let go of the door handle and thought about "the old days." Only weeks ago, I had whole days of solitude ahead of me. I would start outside somewhere, writing nonsense in a notebook, then sit in the library dicking around on the internet, trying to "get into writing mode." Back then I was full of ennui and longing for some sort of structure, but now, after I'd spent six weeks in our tiny fun-house apartment, flailing with Dustin through each exhausting day (and night), all I wanted was to waste time, let my mind wander, listen to music, recover some semblance of an inner life.

"Well, is there any milk?" Dustin said. He opened the fridge in a way that I could only read as accusatory.

"I tried," I told him. I felt like a failure, like a fool. But what was I supposed to do? Breastfeeding was completely supply and demand; my body magically produced the exact amount of milk the baby needed. Maybe I should have been pumping all along, but to add one more chore, one more bodily intrusion? I looked at Dustin with pleading eyes, begging him to have mercy on me.

"You don't know what it's like," Dustin said, his voice quivering now. "You don't hear him scream whenever you leave, even for a few minutes. You can just pull out a boob—"

"*I* don't know what it's like?" I cut him off, exasperated and ready for a fight but painfully aware of the clock ticking. *"Fine,"* I snapped. "I'll be back in an hour." I grabbed my keys and slammed the door when I left. I knew I was being an asshole but as soon as I threw open the door to our building, I no longer cared. I was free. My body felt like a tube of meat with legs and Super Soakers where my breasts should be, but at least the sun was out. I wore sunglasses, leggings, and a T-shirt, my hair unbrushed. I thought about how wild it was that a person could see me and not know why I was so disheveled. I could be anyone. I could be a hungover child. I felt like I should be wearing a sign around my neck. Something like NEW MOTHER. Or CURRENTLY BREASTFEEDING. A scarlet letter *B* so everyone knew my status. At least I was no longer pregnant. *That's something,* I told myself, then put loud music on in my earphones and bounded down our front stoop, feeling like I might cry with happiness. I was rushed but free. Tethered but free. Freer than I'd ever felt when I'd had endless afternoons, no ticking clock.

My reverie was interrupted when I passed my elderly neighbor on his stoop and he shouted after me. "Hey!" he bellowed with real concern, his hands cupped around his mouth. "Where's your baby?" He was wearing a stained undershirt and a bandanna around his neck.

I laughed and spun around to face him, earphones still in. *"With his dad!"* The next time someone asked me that, I swore I'd look around in a panic and start patting my pockets. *My baby? I don't know, have you seen him?*

I'd had only ninety minutes. Now it was eighty-six. It would be eighty by the time I got my coffee and sat down, sixty-five by the time I started working. An hour left after that if you subtracted the time I would need to get back. This math made me want to kick something; it made me feel uncomfortably female. Trapped. But when I got to the corner of the intersection I needed to cross, I found myself leaping out into the street against the Don't Walk sign, darting between parked cars the way I hadn't done in months, in a year, maybe. I flung open the door of the coffee shop and let it sink in: I could leave the house alone now. Get on a train, cross under a river, be in a different part of town from the baby. He was no longer tapping at me from the inside. I could sit in front of my laptop for just under an hour without hearing him cry.

After all that worry during pregnancy about whether I'd be up to the womanly art, breastfeeding had come easily. Or as easily as it could. When the nurse handed the baby to me just twenty minutes after my C-section, I was lying on my back, still shaking from adrenaline and numb from the waist down. I hadn't slept in days. They tucked the tiny shape of him into my armpit, and I, so eager to do the right thing, flopped my gigantic breast out of my hospital gown while everyone looked on. They were a formidable match for each other, my breast and my baby. He attacked it like he was a piranha, knowing better than I did what to do. My job was to just be still, to look at him with admiration, to let relief wash over me—the relief of being met, finally, halfway. He sucked and sucked, needing me like no one ever had before.

He was born knowing. Thank fucking God, this one part had gone right. I marveled at him in his little hat. The nurses clasped their hands together in joy and I beamed back at them, feeling like a good student. It was his first achievement, my first vicarious success.

Within a few hours my proud smile faded into a wince. I sat forward in bed, vigilant, nursing him around the clock, my back aching, my arms shaking with overexertion. Sweat slid down my sides and into the new crevices of my emptied-out and rearranged gut, which was stacked up in a pile beneath my pendulous breasts, my stinging nipples. The nurses came in and out, adjusting him and me. Their advice was all contradictory. I couldn't remember what *The Womanly Art of Breastfeeding* said anymore. Breastfeeding at this point didn't feel like a success so much as an assault, something coming at me faster than I could cope with, happening almost constantly.

Tell me what to do! I wanted to scream. *You do it if you know so much.*

The head nurse came in and moved closer to me, to my sweaty breasts and a floppy baby I wasn't sure how to hold. "It looks like you have the beginnings of an injury," she said, frowning. I didn't know what an injury meant in this case, but I knew I didn't want one on my nipple. I imagined my areola dangling by a thread, like an eye popped out of its socket. My nipple felt bruised and sore. For that first week, my breasts felt like skinned knees that I had to crawl on. I wanted to bandage them up and hide them away but kept having to return them to the hungry fish's mouth, the source of the injury.

That early difficulty made it seem like "figuring things out" was the aim. Mastery. Effort. *Survival.* My nipples healed eventually. My breasts started producing real milk, and the baby stopped losing weight. ("It's normal!" everyone insisted but it didn't feel right, letting your baby waste away

in those first few days before your milk came in.) My arms
and his body grew to meet each other. We did it together.

And then the question quickly shifted from whether or
not I *could* breastfeed to whether or not I *would* do it.
Would I keep going, keep the timer up in my brain, keep
unbuttoning my shirt, keep worrying about what I put into
my body? It was such a straightforward way to feel like a
good mother. I could use it to chase away self-doubt and
know for sure I'd done everything right, done everything
I could. This kind of effort was more reliable to me than
love. It was empirical, actually happening. It was something
I could point to in the middle of the night.

Setting up at a table in my old familiar coffee shop had
me feeling like a person in a long-distance relationship, my
writing and I on one of our rare weekends together. Our
visits would be limited, and between them there was only
longing.

I opened my laptop and immediately felt like a genius.
It turned out writing was easy compared to taking care of a
baby. Writing was something I knew how to do, technically.
No one's life depended on it.

Plus there was no time to procrastinate, not anymore.
No time to get paralyzed second-guessing myself. I'd been
afraid that having a baby would quell whatever ambition
I had, but now the opposite was happening. I'd spent the

past month or so rolling around in the human condition, writing essays in my head, and now I was manic, brimming with things to say. Writing was no longer the most important thing in my life, and that made me love it even more. It was dumb enough to tackle, suddenly; small enough to embolden me. This was it. Maybe this was why I'd had the baby?

I lost track of time, forgetting for a while that I had a body. That is, until my breasts started to tingle and I came back to myself with a jolt. *The baby!* I scrambled to finish the blog post I was working on, hit Publish, slammed my laptop shut, and all but ran home. When my milk came down, I imagined it manifesting as desperate hunger on the other end of some invisible thread between my son and me. The strange twinge I felt when it happened was a little like having to pee but less physically painful. It was like needing to pee emotionally. Like if holding your piss made someone else suffer.

I hurried across the street and down the block and imagined I could hear the baby wailing in our apartment already, Dustin growing more and more furious. My boobs were filling up with milk, hardening and tugging at the skin around my chest. When I finally made it home I threw open the door to the baby crying, just as I'd feared. A wave of guilt passed over me as I grabbed him from Dustin and muttered a string of apologies. (On other days later on, if I got home and he wasn't crying, I'd feel a wave of regret—I should have stayed a few minutes longer. I should have finished my thought.)

As soon as the baby latched on, I burst into tears—of relief, of rage. I'd had this idea of what breastfeeding would be like. Not the physical experience, but the lived reality, the timing, the way it was supposed to fit between other things. I thought it would be something happening in the background while I went about my actual life. How else would it be tolerable? The faint sucking sound of a breast pump during a conference call, a shirt lifted up on the subway, so seamlessly nobody really notices it. Baby legs kicking in the aisle of an airplane, his head and my tits hidden under a gauzy blanket. I wanted to be one of those women who, without missing a beat, pull out a boob at a restaurant, midconversation. That's how they sell it to you: It's so convenient! Always with you. *Natural.* Completely free! "Breastfeeding: It's So Easy!" is how one popular breastfeeding website puts it (every breastfeeder with an internet connection has spent way too many late nights online reading guilt-provoking articles from lactation consultants).

But this easy, natural bodily function took focus, if not on the task at hand, then on the clock. Skip a feed and you mess up the whole supply-and-demand thing. Skip a feed and the milk you didn't express may never show up again, like a friend you cancel on too many times who no longer answers your texts. You can get a clogged milk duct, a painful, inflamed blockage that can then lead to an infection called mastitis, which is like having the flu and then getting stabbed in the tits at the same time. Worse, your baby can "fail to thrive," just quietly starve, without you even knowing it. Your baby's entire nutrition and most of his emotional well-being are completely reliant on your body.

"You know," Dustin said on one endless morning, "you don't have to do it. You can stop any time."

"Ha!" I said. I wasn't sure whether to laugh out loud or cry.

"We'd just give him formula. It would be totally fine. I would be fine with it."

"You have to say that."

"But I mean it!"

I knew I *could* quit any time, even though it didn't feel like that. Not when the Dr. Sears baby manual we had sitting on our coffee table said that breastfeeding on demand was "laying a solid foundation for the person your child would later become." No, I couldn't quit. Not when I had come this far, worked this hard. *Maybe something will happen,* I thought, a secret hope. *Maybe something will happen and my milk will disappear.*

I hated being so on the hook, and I hated that I hated it. To think of myself as genuinely limited, actually held back by breastfeeding, made me feel like a meta-failure.

Considering that breastfeeding was something only I could do for the baby, something I couldn't get a break from without suffering the consequences, it stands to reason that I felt overwhelmed and resentful, but I can see that only now, on the other side of it. At the time, I feared that complaining or admitting how I really felt would make me sound like some unmaternal brat who couldn't submit. Shouldn't I be grateful my body could do it in the first place? All of the books and websites and doctors and nurses and yoga teachers and childbirth instructors insisted that breastfeeding my child for at least a year if not longer was unquestionably worthwhile, and not just for the baby. It was supposed to be its own reward.

Breastfeeding was cheap, always available, and totally portable, argued one of the internet lactation consultants. "Don't give up on one of the most incredible experiences of your life just because you have trouble at first learning a new skill. Give up, and you'll wonder and regret. Persist, and you'll know and be rewarded."

I should have known to be suspicious of the supposed inherent reward of unpaid labor that can be carried out exclusively by the female body (breastfeeding: an unpaid internship you don't get to put on your résumé), but I kept hoping it would come true. Natural childbirth was another supposed "incredible experience," but I had fucked that one up already so there was no way I would give up on breastfeeding (wonder! regret!). I kept waiting for the reward.

I could feel hints of it occasionally, something ancient and primal, an alchemy in the middle of the night. I felt mammalian, like a cavewoman who'd found her life's purpose. *I love you; you need me; I feed you.* It was my shortcut to maternal authority, and for that I was grateful.

The baby up against your body, tugging at you, both of you quiet and still and looking into each other's eyes—it was clear that this intimacy was what we were all trying to get back to. The pleasure and the revelation was fleeting, though. It came on in flashes of contentment and then drifted away when the rest of my life rushed in. The whole world expects you to do it but it's not like it waits for you. People don't accommodate you. They don't even know where to look when you do it.

That whole year I spent as a breastfeeder, I was still myself. I still had ambitions, desires. I was always doing math with the hours, testing the limits of time, trying to see how much living I could get away with. I still had to earn money. I still had to stay sane. Even when it got easier, when the feeds spaced out to every four hours and lasted only five or ten minutes, I couldn't shake the feeling that I was doing something that had been oversold to me, something that was both more difficult and less important than all the books and websites and articles suggested. They had undervalued my time and my sanity. Or was it that they'd overestimated it? I couldn't figure out whether motherhood was showing me how strong I was or how weak. And which one was preferable.

In any case, I did my duty, which was sometimes lovely but more often not. Breastfeeding was not the most incredible experience of my life, and my baby is still mortal. He still gets sick. I went to great lengths to do it, for reasons I can no longer relate to. Or none other than this: I so desperately wanted to do the right thing, and I had no idea what that was yet.

Slacker Parent

IT WAS WHEN we were in that particularly trying window of the first year of parenthood, when the baby was between, say, three and six months old and we expected to be more or less functional and reintegrated back into polite society but were in fact still completely exhausted and adrift, that I developed a theory: Just like there's always someone in a relationship who loves the other person more, there is always one person who is the better parent. By *better*, I mean more enthusiastic, more willing to get down on the rug and play with the blocks, more at home with a baby on his or her hip. I mean that there is one parent who asks the pediatrician questions and argues about sleep training, and there is one who sits there smiling and feeling a little embarrassed.

Do I even need to say it? Dustin was the natural.

Nearly every time we were around other people they

confirmed this dynamic, the women whispering to me about what a great dad he was in this very conspiratorial, female way. Relatives would pat my knee or bump my shoulder with theirs: "Wow, he's so *good* with him." "He's so *engaged*." They'd beam approvingly at Dustin's airplane sounds as he zoomed the baby overhead on the way to the changing table.

I would nod and plaster a smile on my face and say, "I knowwww," trying to make my voice go higher so I wouldn't sound bitter. I was grateful, even if he did make me look bad in comparison. And even if no one batted an eye when I changed a diaper or commented on how "engaged" I was with my child.

Our roles were established in the earliest days. It made sense then, when I was a prisoner to the baby. My body had carried him and birthed him and now sustained him. It stood to reason, I figured, that Dustin would do everything else. And that's how it was. The baby was drinking from my body more often than not, and I, recovering from a C-section, couldn't walk very far or move very quickly, so Dustin flitted about the apartment, compensating for his maleness. Bath time, bedtime, dinnertime, diapers.

It wasn't just chores either. From the beginning Dustin had seemingly endless enthusiasm for lying down on the floor and making animal noises. He was never self-conscious about talking to someone who didn't talk back, like I was (and am). He bought records and danced around the house with our son, and when the baby was fussy he would read to him from books of poetry, Greek myths, and Thomas Hardy novels. I'd stomp through the room rolling my eyes.

Dustin and I used to agree about everything. I used to feel like he saw me and knew me better than anyone. But now that we had a child together, I worried we actually didn't know each other at all. We felt less like a couple than like co-workers, in service to the same human project.

Dustin seemed to have something against the stroller, in-sisting on carrying the baby everywhere himself. "It's not a big deal," he would say, "I like it." When the baby started eating solid foods, Dustin threw himself into steaming ap-ples and carrots and pureeing everything by hand. He fed the baby from a hand-carved wooden bowl that he wanted us to use for every meal and expressed vague disapproval of the baby-food pouches I'd buy at the grocery store. As in "I hate those fucking things."

He was gung-ho about cloth-diapering. "I'm not going to stand over the toilet and scrape shit into it with a wooden spoon anymore!" I declared to the house one morning.

"That's fine," he said. "But I think I'm going to keep do-ing it."

I was baffled. Who was this person swimming laps around me while I was treading water, feeling like I might drown?

And how could I tell him how I felt—how could I trust he'd understand?

I couldn't compete, or didn't want to. I decided if Dustin was going to be obsessed with fatherhood, I would be obsessed with work. We defined ourselves against each other— or I did—like siblings. The amazing father, the good-enough mother. The one who does everything and the one who sits stewing on the couch and lets the baby play with her iPhone (another thing he did not approve of).

On good days I embraced our dynamic, considering it a sort of generational comeuppance. We were both subverting gendered expectations. Think of all the women before me who did everything themselves. Think of all the women now who do everything themselves. (Think of the fathers who did nothing; think of the fathers who *do* nothing.) I deserved to slack off on behalf of those women.

On bad days I wondered what Dustin was trying to prove. On really bad days I took his efforts as criticism, like he was rubbing it in my face: *Look at everything you don't do.* Sometimes I was just so tired, and so angry. *Doesn't he see I was just about to vacuum? Doesn't he see that it doesn't matter if we vacuum? Doesn't he think, like I do, that we deserve a reprieve?*

I used *It's okay, we have a baby* as an excuse for everything. But then Dustin would come in and start wiping the countertops, not looking at me. A rebuke.

He became my superego, a stand-in for the critical voice in my head.

When Anna, an old friend who knew us both well, came to town, she and I hung back on an afternoon walk. She gestured toward Dustin in front of us, carrying the baby on his shoulder, marching and singing.

"Did you see this coming?"

"Yeah. Actually, I did," I told her. Of course I'd seen it coming. Did she think I was a fool? What I hadn't seen coming was me. I'd thought I'd be the same. I thought we'd be equals. What surprised me was my embrace of disposable diapers, my feeling that ease and convenience was now a feminist issue. Doing things the hard way used to be fun, used to be our thing—bake a cake from scratch, bike instead of taking a cab, grow vegetables in the backyard, make zines for everyone for Christmas. But that was when we had ample leisure time and existential angst. Now we were just trying to get through the day.

"What is it about Dustin? Is it just his personality?"

I sighed. I did love him. "I think so. Remember when we had mice in our apartment and he rigged up that elaborate system with the bucket and the two-by-four..."

"Yes! It's the Midwestern part of him," Anna said. Anna was raised in New York.

"Exactly," I said, knowing what she meant. *Midwestern*

conveyed something like "He takes out the trash" and "If the sink is leaking, he will get down there with a flashlight." He always bought toilet paper and milk before we ran out. When we bought a dresser at a stoop sale, he said we should just paint it if we didn't like the color. He was an Eagle Scout. He rode a bike everywhere and carried it up the stairs to our apartment, and that reassured me in some deep-down, probably sexist, taken-care-of way. That sort of thing.

I realized as I talked about him that I was the opposite. That I'd never baked cakes before I met him, that in fact I had made it a point not to learn how to cook. Maybe under the stress of new parenthood, whatever adult personality I'd concocted was being stripped for parts, and I would be left with only my teenage core. It was like the opposite of our early courtship, when I was on all the time and vigilantly trying to be my best self, to be charming and laid back, someone worthy of his affection.

Anna turned to me. "Do you love him even more now?"

"No!" I said without thinking. Anna didn't say anything and I worried I was disappointing her. I knew what the answer should have been: *Seeing him with our child makes me love him more than I ever thought possible.* I knew I was—we were—so lucky, but when I watched them together, I felt more relieved than grateful. It made me want to slip away, go do something I was good at.

He was the good dad. I was just the default mom. "I

mean, equality is great and all in theory," I told Anna, "but it just means we have to discuss everything. No one's the authority. *He has a temperature. What should we do? Should we give him Tylenol? Call the pediatrician? Who's gonna call?* Then he second-guesses me. As if I don't do that enough on my own. I think with other people, the mom just pretends to know, and the dad gets to play the idiot in the background."

"But you wouldn't want it that way, would you?"

I wouldn't, it was true. But it would be nice to be the one who *knew*. The expert. The mom.

I didn't want to tell Anna about the fantasy I entertained on days when I got really annoyed (when I was convinced, say, that Dustin was sweeping the floor only to make me feel bad): that if he weren't there, I would rise to the occasion. I'd have to. I'd get a real job and put the baby in day care. Let him cry it out at night. Give him the pouches of baby food Dustin hates without anyone there to judge me.

I'd do it alone and get all the credit. And not feel like a child, grumbling and tired and weak, needing to be taken care of—parented. Motherhood made me so vulnerable. He had taken care of me and the baby like I knew he would. Of course he had. But part of me felt like I'd never catch up.

Anna and I climbed the steps back into our house; it was time to feed the baby. Dustin may have been the good parent, but I was still the mother. For better or worse, I had the breasts and the uterus and the mom-smell, and when Anna and I sat down on the couch, my child practically leaped out of Dustin's arms and into mine. Dustin's competence made me feel insecure but I knew that no matter what I did, the baby would still be obsessed with me, his food source. As long as I was breastfeeding, we were best friends, joined at the tit, never away from each other for more than a few hours. When the baby looked up at me from the changing table, I could swear he saw into my soul. No judging, no preconceived notions, no assumptions, just seeing, and loving, and there. It was so intimate I could barely stand to stare back.

We all took off our shoes, and the baby and I settled into the couch. Anna sat on the living-room floor across from us, taking in the scene from below. "You're a mom!" she said, like it was still surreal.

I laughed and turned a little red, still unused to the word. Maybe that was part of my problem. Dustin had embraced fatherhood but I couldn't bring myself to say *mama* out loud, not until my son did. It was embarrassing; it felt goofy or fake. Who wanted to be a mother, anyway? *Mom* called to mind a relationship with someone, not an individual. A mom was your servant. A mom picked up the wrong thing at the supermarket. A mom needed to stop and get stamps on the way home from soccer practice and you hated her for it. A mom wore a white, collared shirt and stood at the kitchen island selling cereal in television commercials. Moms clustered on benches in the playground pulling snacks out of their bags. They took up the whole sidewalk with their goddamn strollers. Moms nagged. Moms were stressed out. I knew it was all internalized misogyny and guilt and bad public policy but I still couldn't really get around it. There was no mother I wanted to be. I wanted to be myself, but better. I wanted to be the type of person who woke up before the baby and went for a run. This was what my mother did with us. To me, this was what a mother was: someone who was one step ahead of everyone, who had her finger on the pulse of the household, who came in with groceries just when you wondered where she was.

This was exactly what I wasn't.

"So, have you met any other moms?" Anna asked me, gently prodding. "Joined some kind of group?"

"No," I admitted. "I mean, not really." I had figured that eventually I'd get over myself and make all kinds of mom friends naturally. They would be real people, not stereotypes. A mom and I would share a look at the playground and I'd compliment her on her tattoo and make a joke and then soon enough we'd be sipping tea in her kitchen. We'd take turns consoling and complimenting each other in equal measure. Our babies, of course, would be napping in the next room.

But that hadn't happened yet, and so what? I already had friends. Real friends, ones who got my jokes and who I didn't have enough time for as it was. Friends like Anna, people who were watching with interest while I lived out this strange experiment.

"Don't you think it would be helpful? You know, to have someone to talk to who gets it?"

"Ugh. Probably," I conceded just as Dustin rushed in to grab the baby, who had fallen asleep in my arms mid–nursing session. He carried him on one forearm, swaying a little as he climbed the stairs to lay his little body in the crib. We could hear him humming "Baby Beluga" from upstairs. Anna's eyes got big and she pointed up at the ceiling like *Who is this guy?* I shrugged and tucked my legs under me on the couch, trying not to seem impressed.

The next morning Anna and her boyfriend flew back to San Francisco, and I spotted a woman from prenatal yoga at our neighborhood coffee shop. I was surprised at how happy I was to see her; I felt like I'd just run into a crush at the mall. Somehow, unlike me, she looked just as beautiful as she had the last time I'd seen her, when we stood on a street corner after yoga class and confessed to each other how scared we were about childbirth. I had promised to send her an e-mail once the baby came, but I never did.

"Are you going to story time at the library today?" she asked me. She was about a foot taller than me and had big brown eyes; she looked formidable but kind as she navigated her stroller around the crowd of people waiting for their drinks.

"Oh, I dunno," I said. "Dustin's taken the baby but I've never been. I've seen the moms going in when I'm there trying to get work done, but it seemed really intimidating!"

She laughed at me. "It's just nice to get out of the house, you know?" she said. "It's something to do."

I texted Dustin my new plan and, surprising myself, went home to grab the baby. *Here I am,* I thought, *turning over a new leaf. I'm open, receptive. Maybe next I'll start exercising.*

I recognized some of the moms from yoga and my childbirth classes, and the ones I didn't sized me up, and I them. I mouthed *Hi* and, flushed, pulled a chair up to a distinct group of women with babies my son's age. They seemed to know one another well; they must have been coming to story time for weeks. They scooted their chairs closer—begrudgingly, I felt—making room for me. I hated all of them immediately. The singing had already started so I unclipped the carrier and bounced my infant on my lap and wondered if I should do the gestures for "The Wheels on the Bus." Should I stomp his feet for "If You're Happy and You Know It" or should I stomp my own?

"Do we have to stand up?" I whisper-shouted to the woman sitting next to me. She shot me a weird look.

"You don't have to do anything!" she said, and then she quickly jumped up and tossed her baby into the air, laughing with what appeared to be real joy. I sat there feeling self-conscious, trying to muster an excited face to make at my kid, who was too busy being sensory-overloaded to notice me. *This is hell,* I thought. My armpits got hot and tingled and I screamed in my head, feeling like a teenager again or like a child in gym class. I felt new. I was new.

When the story ended, it was time for all the kids to play together. Of course that was impossible; our babies were newborns, stuck flopping around on our laps. Playtime was for the moms to interact, to make polite conversation. When you are the mother of a new baby, however, polite conversation is typically a desperate grasp at information: How does your child nap, how does he eat, what brand of diapers do you use? The trick is to answer questions honestly but be ready to disavow whatever you do if, compared to the other person's routine, it's too strenuous or too laid back. The fantasy is meeting another parent who does the exact same things you do so you don't have to question or defend any of it.

In the library basement, I found no one like me. No one hated it enough. No one else felt suicidal, desperate for a drink. One woman—wearing glittery slip-on shoes and bright leggings that showed off her still-round tummy— was clearly the leader. She asked for my e-mail so that she could add me to the group. "Look at that neck control!" she shouted over the din, pointing at my baby. I panicked. Her own kid was a lump, falling sideways. "How many weeks is he?"

I fought the urge to lie and say he was older. I didn't need any of these women resenting me for my son's advanced motor skills. "How is he sleeping?" she asked me.

"Terribly," I said, hoping to make up for the neck thing. When someone commented on how cute he was, I caught myself pointing out how he didn't have any hair. I was self-deprecating on behalf of my baby. Not yet four months old and he was already a victim of my insecurity.

When the ringleader excused herself to go talk to someone else, I found myself sitting alone with the baby on my lap. I looked around the room without making eye contact with anyone, lonelier than I'd been before I'd gotten there. I sat there feeling ugly, and embarrassed, a gray stack of flesh in cotton jersey. My body I'd expected to be a crime scene, but even my face looked bad lately. My hair was the color of dishwater and I put it up, still wet, in a ponytail every morning. Even when I wore makeup, I looked, and felt, like I'd had the life drained out of me. I tried to seem busy, playing with my own baby while I listened to the women around me hungrily interrogate one another. They were explaining their daily schedules in precise detail. *How long does she nap? Does she take three naps or just two? Does she nap in the stroller or in your lap or in the crib or the carrier? Does he drink three ounces of pumped milk at a time or four ounces? I mean, I don't even know, I exclusively breastfeed. Were you going to go back to work at six weeks or eight? I don't think I'm going to go back to work at all. I have to. I love that onesie. Isn't it perfect. Is it from Carter's? Carter's for Target or Carter's-Carter's?*

I felt as hungry for the minutiae of their circumscribed days as they were but I was also filled with self-loathing for caring at all. We sounded so desperate, we moms. So boring. *Can you believe this is what our lives have been reduced to?* I wanted to say. *Remember when we were real people? Remember feeling in charge of your life?*

I looked around one last time, then, feeling overwhelmed with sadness, I clipped the carrier around my waist while balancing the baby precariously on my lap, zipped up his tiny hoodie, nestled him onto my chest, and put my arms through the straps. I kissed his head. He'd ruined my life but I loved him. I didn't hold it against him.

I looked right, looked left, and darted up the stairs. The library was full of regular people reading books and doing work. I hurried past them and out the door. *I just wanted a baby,* I thought. *I don't want to be a mother. I want to be a writer. I want to be taken seriously. I want money. I want more time. I want to lose weight. I want to be beautiful. I want a day completely to myself, though I don't even remember what I used to do with them when days to myself were a thing I had.*

* * *

When I got home I collapsed onto the bed to feed the baby while Dustin orbited around the fixed point of us. "Hi, *family!*" he said, with extra emphasis on *family*. Was that what we were? He gathered us in his arms and I groaned. Just as I was not a mother yet, we were definitely not a family, not to me. The word felt corny and forced. I wanted to kick it away and claim the word for myself only when I was good and ready. When I was in a better mood. When I felt more worthy of it.

"So?" Dustin said, searching. "How was it?"

"You know. Dumb," I said.

"Aw, come on. I think it's nice! The lady that does the songs—"

"Yeah, you didn't tell me there was *singing* involved. Jesus Christ."

He laughed and got back up to finish making dinner.

"Do you talk to anyone when you go?" I asked him.

"No. I mean, I don't know. I don't *not* talk to people. I just hang out with our guy here."

"You mean you didn't meet *the moms?* Oh my God. It's such a scene."

He laughed, admitted he had no idea what I was talking about. I envied him that. No one suggested he make dad friends. He got to demolish low expectations of fatherhood

161

while I got defensive. I feared being eaten alive by motherhood, being completely subsumed. He seemed light-years away from me right then. Even his love for me was confusing. I didn't feel worthy of that either.

I wanted to arrive by our new happiness honestly, without trying to, at some later date. I wanted it to be undeniable, to take us by surprise. A mother, a father, a baby, a family. I would be happy despite myself. I would wake up before my family and go for a run. Before that, though, I wanted someone to come along and agree that yes, everything was shit. I so wanted that person to be him.

Instead, he came back over to sit on the edge of the bed and make joyful noises at us, kissing my cheek, my neck, my ear, as I stiffened against him and begged him, in my mind, not to say it. He did anyway: "My *family!*" It occurred to me that, oh, maybe he already *was* happy. Maybe the trying was what did it for him, what made parenting click for him so much sooner than it did for me. Maybe it was that he had the freedom to try, to make an effort, to choose to show up.

Whether it was working or not, I could see that he was trying for me—for all of us. He was grabbing at the good parts of what we had and hanging on. Maybe he knew we couldn't both fall apart. Maybe he could see that I needed it to be my turn. I needed to be able to fall apart. I needed to come to all of it in my own time. And until then, someone had to make dinner.

Maternal Instincts

FOR THE FIRST few weeks I was always expecting to catch the baby, somehow, mid-death. If Dustin wasn't watching me, I sat on the edge of our bed staring, my breath stopping when the baby's did, my mind counting the seconds until he gasped, his tummy like a small balloon, filling up. I hovered over him, vigilant, while he slept, watching the reassuring rise and fall of his chest. During the day I puttered around the apartment, inventing reasons to walk by his bassinet and confirm he was still alive. It felt like this was what I was born to do: save my son just as he was slipping away forever, shake him awake before he left us and fell back to wherever it was he came from.

When we left the house with the baby nestled on Dustin's chest in one of those elaborate fabric baby wraps, I would stop Dustin every few minutes to peek in, check he hadn't suffocated. When we took the baby to lie on a blanket in the park, I knelt next to him, my eyes darting left and right, watching to make sure a bird or a squirrel didn't swoop in and attack his face. I knew I was being ridiculous by any objective standards, or so went some paternal voice in my head, some superego mix of Dustin and a stern pediatrician.

The human body is a miraculous thing. Babies are resilient! He's fine! He's fine! He's fine!

At night, whether he was crying or not, I woke up every hour or so with a gasp and shone the light of my phone over his face, put my fingers under his nose to feel for breath.

I knew that if the unthinkable—which is to say, the thing I couldn't stop thinking about—happened, I would regret not staying awake all night with a flashlight pointed at his tiny chest, watching him breathe. My vigilance would seem worth it, unquestionably. Was this not my responsibility? My role? My body had built his body cell by cell by cell, spent almost a year putting him together in the dark, and now I was supposed to sit back and tend to him, keep him safe and alive with my milk but also—impossibly, it felt— trust that his body would do its work, that he would keep breathing all on his own.

I think it must have started in the hospital. In order for me to be discharged after the baby was born, there were a few things we had to accomplish. Forms to sign. Pamphlets to read. Hospital surveys to fill out. Dustin's paternity to declare, since we weren't married. I was supposed to take a shower, take a shit, be able to walk around on my own.

Then, last of all, there was the SIDS video. "Did you watch the video yet?" the nurses kept asking me, a little apologetic. "They make us tell you to. There's a quiz you have to take."

Sudden infant death syndrome. The leading cause of death for infants and a catchall term for the rare but distinct and haunting possibility that your child could die at any moment for no discernible reason. Everyone said there was no use ruminating on it because you couldn't ever fully prevent it, you couldn't control it, but then you were told not to co-sleep, not to put blankets in the baby's crib, not to let him sleep on his stomach, as if to remind you that although you couldn't guarantee that your child wouldn't die—in fact, he surely would one day, as would we all—you were responsible for doing everything you could to make sure he didn't. You couldn't prevent death, but you could contribute to causing it. It might be your fault. Especially if you broke one of the rules from the video.

"Oh," I said, caught off guard. "No, I haven't done it yet," I said, "but I think I know the gist," which was a vast understatement. I could have given a lecture on SIDS to the National Institutes of Health, though all of my findings would have been horror stories posted on various internet forums that I'd sought out and read in the middle of the night just to torture myself.

Of course I aced the quiz, which went over the central tenets of the Back to Sleep campaign, started in the mid-1990s to encourage parents to put infants to sleep on their backs. The quiz had trick questions like "What kind of blanket should you put in the crib?" Answer: *None,* because the blanket could cover his face and he could suffocate. No pillows either. No loose clothing. The baby should sleep in the same room as you but *not* in your bed or on your chest as you're rocking him in the middle of the night, only half awake yourself. Pacifiers help lower the risk of "dying in infancy of an unknown cause," which was another way to say SIDS. Breastfeeding helps too. Maternal smoking is a risk factor for SIDS. As are pregnancy complications and premature birth. I had the list memorized but still Googled it on occasion to feel a sort of selfish reassurance that we would be spared. As in: *Phew, my baby loves his pacifier, so it will be someone else, some other poor parent.* As if there were a quota of babies who would die and mine was not one of them. At least for now. Not yet.

Even now, when I think of the term *SIDS* and look up the statistics, I hold my breath without meaning to, start to feel dizzy. I think of all the parents who do everything right and whose babies still die mysteriously in their cribs, on their backs. And I think of the parents who do the wrong thing, whether out of desperation or ignorance or defiance. I think of one family whose story I read in the middle of an anxiety-fueled night: *We do not believe our son died because he was sleeping on the couch with his dad,* one mother wrote, or something like that. Then she added that, while there was no way to know for sure, they had chosen to believe that their child would have died that night anyway, and they took comfort in the knowledge that he hadn't spent his last moments alone. I think of all the times I fell asleep with the baby on my chest without meaning to. You just get so tired.

The Back to Sleep campaign has decreased SIDS deaths by 50 percent in the decade-plus it's been around. It's been a success, undeniably. But taking the quiz felt like touching the void. It made the truth impossible to ignore or repress: Death was inextricable from life. Our real task was not-killing a small, precious thing.

The macabre was everywhere, once I started looking. *Breathability* was advertised on all the baby products we bought, a word that used to mean fabric that didn't cause a yeast infection but now referred to the lifesaving mesh in the sides of the bassinet or playpen. The baby's crib came with a big warning about keeping it away from window blinds to avoid strangulation. I read it and froze where I was standing, visions of my baby, stiff and blue, flashing through my mind. Which I guess was the point. Thank God it was summer, so the omnipresent receiving blankets were all thin cotton. Even so, they were treacherous, like every other object. I imagined them falling into his crib in the middle of the night, inching up around his mouth like pythons as he slept, taking him from us in an instant.

One afternoon I was playing peekaboo with the baby, one of the blankets over my face, and Dustin caught me making a covert attempt to see if I could breathe through it. Just to test it.

"What're you doing?" he said.

"Nothing! Whatever."

"I did it too," he admitted. I exhaled. Dustin was my standard of normalcy. I'd always harbored an obsession with death, or a too-keen awareness that it was coming for all of us, so I didn't really trust my own brain. "Ever since you were a kid," my mom would say, shaking her head. "I have no idea where you got it from." I used to convince myself that my mom would get murdered on one of her long morning runs. Or that there was cancer hidden somewhere in my body. Or hers. I would lie in bed writing the story in my head, preemptively feeling guilty for all the bad things I wrote about her in my diary.

When I got older I imagined getting hit by a bus. Thrown onto the subway tracks. A brain aneurysm. Then once I met Dustin, or once I fell in love with him, my death fantasies transferred to him. Anytime he didn't pick up his phone, he was obviously lying dead on the side of the road, run over by a semi while he rode his bike. Attacked when he left work late at night. Or he'd slipped and fallen while he cleaned our kitchen floor, been impaled by the mop. I guess I should have seen the baby-dying fear coming.

But even now, in hindsight, my fear seems rational to me. Infants lack the solidity of grown people, the layers of years lived and personality accrued—all the trappings that distract you from the horrible vulnerability a baby arrives with: a neck that bends in just a way to remind you of the arteries, the critical nerves, inside it; a nearly bald skull covered in nauseating blue veins, visible and running over the tops of the ears. The baby's soft spot right at the crown of his head, no hair to hide the place where the skull has yet to fuse together, and—the worst part—it pulses with his heartbeats at odd intervals, as if to scream, *I am just a mortal body,* over and over.

Dustin thought the pulsing soft spot was funny. "It's doing the thing again."

"Ugh!" I couldn't look away even though looking made me feel ill. I would do an exaggerated shudder, trying to shake off the horror like a dog shakes off water.

The more that people, especially Dustin, dismissed my fears, the less I trusted them. *Babies do die,* I wanted to say to everyone. I felt like sending them links to tragic blog posts. *Don't you see what we're dealing with here?* I would tell them.

You think this is all elephant onesies and hooded towels, but it's a matter of life and death!

It's no one's fault, people would have said if it had happened. But they might not have meant it.

I knew I wouldn't have believed them. If the baby died, I'd have to answer to everyone, answer to myself as a mother. It was knowing that I would feel culpable forever, no matter what, that took my breath away. I tried playing out the worst-case scenario in my mind, hoping that confronting it would sap some of its power (nope). I'd push the stroller around the neighborhood thinking, *Okay, so we would be very sad. Broken.* Our lives would be defined by tragedy, just like the lives of all the people I'd read about on the internet, the ones whose babies had been born with severe birth defects or had been in terrible accidents or hadn't survived birth. But eventually my life would go back to what it was like pre-baby. We'd travel. Sleep late again. I'd write about it. In a way, the baby dying was more fathomable than him living. That we were falling deeply in love, that the stakes were higher than they'd ever been before, and we would have to live with it, with loving like this—that was harder to take in than the possibility of a great tragedy.

I read a story on a parenting forum around this time that described my dark fantasy to a tee. A woman was at a parade with her children. She had her newborn in a stroller covered by a thin blanket so that the baby could nap in peace while she tended to the rest of her family. Suddenly, or so she wrote, something came over her, some intuition, and she rushed over to the stroller, flung off the blanket, and crouched down to stare at her son. She squinted at him, watching his chest for movement, and saw nothing. Without stopping to think, she reached out to him and shook him awake. As she told it, this caused him to startle, open his eyes wide, and gasp for air.

"I saved my baby's life," she wrote. "I'm sure of it." She was clearly still shaken, as was everyone else reading about it on the forum, up all night with their own inscrutable infants. "I don't even want to think what would have happened if I hadn't run over to him," she said. People wrote, *Thank God,* and said they'd hug their babies closer that night. (But not too close.) The image of the baby, shaken awake, taking in a huge gasp of air, played on a loop in my head, though even at the time I didn't really believe she'd saved her baby's life. *Sleep apnea,* I argued, trying to reassure myself, or maybe he was simply between breaths. What really plagued me was the decisive, intuitive action of the mother, who'd put down her paper plate of potato salad or corn on the cob or whatever it was to go running over to her son.

It was that gut feeling, the same one that would send me, a little quicker than necessary, over to peer into the baby's bassinet. What if, when it came down to it, I didn't get the feeling? Or what if I had to stop listening to the feeling because it kept overfiring, and then, as soon as I stopped, as soon as I relaxed, the bad thing happened? What if my gut feelings—*Something bad has happened!*—were simply anxiety, simply hormones, simply the result of too many tragic stories I had tried to hold in my brain and live through, as if an act of radical empathy could spare me, render me immortal? What if I couldn't be trusted? What's neurosis and what's maternal instinct?

I knew, though, that if I listened to every bad feeling, it would take over my mind. I'd never do anything else. I would be pulling the car over every time I called out to him and he, an infant who couldn't say words yet, didn't answer. *You're being ridiculous,* I would tell myself. *He's fine.* I'd keep driving, then think, *But what if he is dead?* And then for the rest of my life I'd think about how I sat there with my gut feeling and ignored it.

And so I would try to watch myself as if from a distance. I would observe the panic rising up in me when, say, the light shifted and the baby's face looked a disturbing shade of gray. Was he smiling at me but secretly suffocating? Would I know it if I saw it? I can still feel it in my neck, adrenaline shooting out from wherever, tension rising up my neck, a jolt of dread in my solar plexus, and a ringing in my ears before I snatched him up in my arms and held him under a different light and then caught my breath, happy to know it was just me, just my awful brain.

* * *

When the baby started crawling, I was afraid he'd fall down the stairs. When he started walking, that he'd wander into traffic. For a while I was convinced he would fall off the porch, go rolling down the cement front steps and onto the sidewalk and then into the road just as a car came flying down the street. I imagined boiling pasta water spilling onto his face, a knife falling from the counter and landing in some unspeakably unlucky area of his tiny body. I saw neck-breaking falls from playground equipment, even when Dustin had taken him and I was at home unloading the dishwasher. I saw all these scenarios in vivid flashes, as if they were in a movie. I'd try to shake them out of my head. I'd squeeze my eyes shut sometimes. My breath would catch.

Dustin maintained that I was crazy, but on the rare nights we went on dates that first year, I'd see he was a little crazy too. We only ever went out when a family member was in town, when we had no real excuse not to. We knew it was a good idea to go. To "reconnect." Then we'd both sit there at the restaurant, checking our phones throughout dinner.

"He's probably not dead, right?" he'd ask.

"Nah," I'd say, happy to play the chill parent for once. "She would have called if he died." Dustin would nod and try to change the subject but I'd stare off into space, panic growing. I imagined the baby dying at that very moment and us thinking about the irony of our conversation for the rest of our lives.

"Well, I'll just text and check in," I'd say, hiding my phone under the table, blushing from the wine.

After we came home from dinner one such night—the restaurant was just around the corner, within running distance, *just in case*—I chatted with Dustin's sister, Piper, while Dustin walked into our living room, where the baby was asleep in the crib. I wanted desperately to rush over to him, just to look at him, to visually confirm he had survived the hour without us. But like so many other times, in the interest of appearing sane, I fought my urge. I rinsed out a bottle of breast milk, asked Piper how she'd been, trying to act cool. Dustin came back into the kitchen. "How is he?" I asked.

"He's alive," Dustin said, putting his arm around me, knowing that was my real question. I couldn't take it anymore and slipped out from under his arm and rushed to go check on the baby, fearing the word *alive* was tempting fate. "You're not going to like what you see!" Dustin called after me.

I leaned over the crib and gasped. The baby was lying facedown, his arms by his sides, looking like a corpse. He was breathing, not to mention sound asleep, but I grabbed him out of the crib anyway, adrenaline rushing through me. "Mama's here," I said to him, using that word out loud for the first time and feeling it, too, as if my vulnerability were what called the name, the role, into being.

I didn't know before that when parents talked about "checking on" their children, they meant checking to make sure they weren't dead. And when they talked about their love for their children, maybe that was what they meant too. It was love but keener, with sharper edges, softer undersides. It was love wrapped up with desperate terror, inextricable.

That spring, when the baby was nine months old, my sister visited us from Chicago. At that point, the baby was sitting and clapping and doing a funny crawl, one where he pushed his body forward with one foot—like lizard pose in yoga, his foot flat on the ground—the other leg trailing behind. He was joyful. He was bald, strangely attentive and perceptive, and starting to talk. He sat in my sister's lap and grinned at her, reaching for her hair. We decided that first morning she was there that we were going to go out to breakfast, where our son would bounce on our laps and eat small fistfuls of biscuit.

On the way out the door, I started to buckle the baby carrier around my waist and then stopped myself. "Do you want to carry him?" I asked my sister. Younger sisters usually love this sort of thing; anything for a photo they can post on Facebook.

She said no, she didn't want to wear the carrier. I was taken aback. *"Why not?"*

She started walking ahead of us and then spun around, shrugging. "I've always been afraid of falling over wearing one of those things—like, what if you fell forward on top of the baby?" She laughed like she knew she was being ridiculous but also like she wanted to make sure we'd considered this possibility.

I waved the thought away. Dustin had been over the same thing with me before. "You're extra-aware when you have it on," I said. "Plus, when have you ever fallen *forward*, onto your face? That doesn't happen." Anyway, Dustin was the one who usually carried the baby. He was the man, after all, and therefore stronger. It made sense in my head, in a subconscious way, like how I always slid into the passenger seat before a long trip without offering to drive.

After breakfast, though, I started putting on the carrier. "You're taking him?" Dustin said.

"Yeah," I said with a slight attitude, "clearly." He had been off bussing our tray and I'd figured I might as well take the opportunity to display some maternal authority for my sister.

On the short walk home from breakfast, the sun came out and we sang "The Ants Go Marching" out loud. Couples walked past us on the sidewalk holding hands, probably headed down the main drag to the same place for biscuits. I was thinking about what a beautiful day it was when my Dansko clog caught on an edge of the sidewalk. My body resisted gravity at first, and I started waving my arms in the air like a tightrope walker trying to balance herself. I think I took another galloping step.

I have a clear memory of time slowing down. I remember thinking, *No, no, no,* as I flew forward in the air, and then I realized that if I pretended it wasn't happening, the fall would be worse, but if I accepted the fact that I was going to fall, I could try to fall well. I could see my sister and Dustin standing there, not quite getting what was happening. I willed my whole body to turn in midair and flung my left shoulder back, twisting thirty degrees to the right, so that instead of falling flat on my face, I would land on my side.

I did it somehow; I spun in the air, and my right hip and shoulder hit the ground first. I had hugged the baby to me in the carrier on the way down but he was wailing. I started crying too. He had a giant scrape on his head, but I insisted he hadn't hit the ground. Dustin ran the few steps over to us and quickly unbuckled the carrier. "Give him to me," he said.

"How did you do that?" my sister said in awe. I slowly staggered to my feet and pulled pebbles and dirt out of my hand.

"I don't even know!" I was flabbergasted, terrified. I tried to get a closer look at the baby. "Is he okay?" I said, desperate.

"He's fine," Dustin said, pulling him out of my sight. "You have to promise never to wear those shoes again, okay? Not around the baby."

"Okay," I said, stung. Of course it had been me. *But my heroism!* I wanted to say. *The twist! I bent our fate! I intervened!* Then again, it was still my fault. I fell. The baby was hurt and I was responsible. But wasn't I, who had given him life, responsible for everything?

Dustin held the baby and we resumed singing "The Ants Go Marching," not stopping until we were home, and at some point he stopped crying and all of us calmed down. *Maybe all it takes is distraction. For you and the baby, for everyone. Think about other things. Stop thinking about all the bad things that could happen. Not because they can't happen but because it's the only way to calm down.*

I looked at the baby and at the scrape on his head that Dustin let me believe was a sort of rug burn from the baby carrier. I felt sick to my stomach but hugely relieved. Something lifted then, if temporarily. The bad thing had happened and the baby had survived. He could be hurt without dying. He could endure my mistakes. He was vulnerable but resilient. Human. Wasn't that the problem, in the end? He was going to walk around in the world where there were a million different ways to die. One day something would kill him. And I loved him too much for that. And yet. What else is there to say?

Dry Spell

IT WAS LUNCHTIME on February 13, and Dustin and I were about to do our midday baby handoff. I had been working in a coffee shop and he'd spent the morning at the park with the baby; now it was my turn to take over. I tried to blot out all the opinions and ambition and worldly attachment I'd spent the past three or four hours trying to get back in touch with as I climbed the stairs to our front porch.

The next day would be our first Valentine's Day together as parents, a fact to which I'd been assigning increasing, and arbitrary, meaning. For weeks I'd been writing *valentine's day????* on a to-do list in my phone but had yet to make any real plans or take any action. Would I get it together and write a love letter, bake a cake, make a print of the baby's feet inside a heart, and prove to myself and whoever followed me on Instagram that Dustin and I were still as in love as ever?

For Valentine's Days past, there'd been pipe-cleaner hearts, love notes written with shower crayons bought special for the occasion, junk-store postcards tucked into the perfect book (Eileen Myles, Mavis Gallant, Colette). There was the year he hid each individual chocolate from a box in a different place around our small apartment; months later, I'd be looking for a cough drop or a cigarette and laugh out loud when I found one. If I could only pull something like that off, then I'd know things were still the same between us, or would be eventually.

I opened the door and found the two of them at the kitchen table, the baby kicking in the high chair, smearing applesauce everywhere, Dustin reading aloud to him from *Paradise Lost*. I rolled my eyes but felt a piercing affection for them. My family. I got a washcloth to wipe down the table, then grabbed the baby and slumped down on the couch with him, breathing him in.

If you'd asked me the day before, I would have said that the baby and I were going to spend the afternoon doing some kind of last-minute romance craft, but now that the occasion was upon us, that seemed a little too ambitious. God. What was it like, to do a nice thing for someone that wasn't obligatory? I could remember the gestures, even remember how nice they felt, but I could no longer relate to the impulse. As I nursed the baby, I whittled down the plan. *Okay,* I thought, *I'll get up early with the baby tomorrow and then we'll...make a cute breakfast. I'll have him draw on a card.*

Dustin's plan, I was sure of it, started and ended with him having sex with me. Or so I was dreading.

Maybe that's what I was hoping to compensate for: *I love you, I think. Sorry for all the sexual rejection.* I felt bad about it. Sort of. I knew it was hurting him. And yet. That February and for the entire year or so postpartum—when do you stop being postpartum? Or are you that way forever?—I not only didn't want to have sex, I would have preferred it not exist.

I knew our whole dynamic was threatening to move from sitcom territory into an actual problem, a problem that could be fixed, or at least de-escalated, by my just getting on with it. Lie back without thinking too much, fake it till you make it, you know the drill. And I did do it every month or so, after endless internal debate. Sometimes it felt good, too, in the end, but it was preceded by so much anxious hand-wringing it never felt quite worth it. Couldn't we put sex on the back burner for a while? Revisit when the mood strikes?

The mood was always striking him, never me, and that was the problem. We were going on nine months since the birth and I still felt like punching him when he poked me in the butt with his erection before we fell asleep. It seemed like we were doomed sex-wise, or I was, which meant we were doomed relationship-wise, which meant we were painstakingly building a life together that wasn't going to go anywhere ultimately. And how would that even work? It wouldn't. We'd have to figure it out. Or I would.

"How was the park?" I said out loud to the house, sensing Dustin in my peripheral vision. I wanted to know every detail of what our son had done while I was gone, everything I missed.

"Oh, good. We chased crows. Stared at the grass. He went down the big slide." I felt a pang of jealousy as I pulled up my shirt to breastfeed the baby. I wondered if maybe I should try taking him in the mornings. Maybe Dustin had the better deal.

When Dustin started putting on his boots to go out instead of going upstairs to work like he usually did, I looked at him like he was suiting up for a trip to the moon. "Where are you going?" I tried to keep my voice neutral but could hear myself veering into the accusatory.

"Oh, I thought I'd do some shopping." He threw a paperback into his tote bag and paced around the house, getting a drink of water, grabbing his coat.

"I just went to the grocery store yesterday!" I called to him in the kitchen, meaning *Hello? What is wrong with you?*

"No, not that kind of shopping."

I looked at him funny. "Where, then? For what?"

"So curious," he said in his infuriating way.

I made a face at him from my perch on the couch, the

baby still feeding. "Speaking of, have you, uh, gotten me anything for Valentine's Day yet?"

I wondered whether he'd give me the Speech tonight, the one he tended to whisper at me, gently, when I turned my back to him and stared at the wall, wishing I could disappear into the bedcovers. "Eventually," he'd say, stroking my hair while the rest of me tensed up, "you're going to remember that you like sex."

The baby finished nursing and Dustin was still looking for the perfect book to carry around in his tote bag and not read while he was out.

"So, did you?" I asked again. "Get me anything yet?"

"Well—" he said.

Suddenly my uneasiness shifted into relief. "Me either!" I shouted after him, jubilant. "Hey!" I felt so close to him then, in some sort of sad state of grace. I stood up and carried the baby over to where he was. "Maybe we should come with you? We could all go together, pick out what we want?"

I sat in the back of the car, next to the car seat in case of emergency (aka the baby crying), while Dustin drove. I tried to get comfortable in my raincoat and too-tight jeans, avoiding my reflection in the rearview mirror. I felt disgusting. But it was nice out, at least, and the baby was wearing this very cute yellow hat that made him look like an elf. I played with his toes. "What do you want for Valentine's Day anyway?" I shouted over the music. This question was an act of aggression, I knew. Thinking of something to want, summoning enough desire to be able to say it out loud—that was the hardest part.

"You know what I want," he said predictably in his suggestive '80s rom-com voice, an answer that by now had become routine.

"Ha!" I said, and let my head fall back onto the seat.

"It's not a joke," he said, trying to make eye contact in the rearview mirror, both hands on the steering wheel.

"Oh, I know." I tensed up thinking of him coming over to me to kiss my shoulder as soon as I put the baby down to sleep that night, his face in my face as soon as I had the chance to pull up Twitter on my phone. "Hi," I would say, trying to acknowledge him but still staring at my screen. I'd kiss him a little and then go back to whatever I was reading and he would come at me again. "Come on," he would probably say, at which point I would have to do a quick internal review. The question was not *Do I want it?* so much as *Do I have it in me to endure it?* If I waved him away, he'd pout or, worse, get shitty and sulk, pass by me on the couch the next day without acknowledging my existence. I'd feel terrible but not bad enough to fuck him.

We drove up and down the main drag looking for parking. The side streets were lit up with the sun, front porches and old-fashioned windows and bright colors. I knew I loved Dustin still, even though I was unhappy. I knew we had been very happy once, and I had staked my life on the blind belief we would stay that way.

Dustin and I met when he was working a closing shift at my neighborhood bookstore. He knew who I was because the store was carrying an anthology about sex I'd recently edited, *Coming and Crying*. He wrote a small post on his blog about my essay, referring to me as O'Connell and praising my writing. Small detail: The piece was about the time I had sex with someone in the bathroom stall of a bar. I guess you could say that set a tone.

I did miss, if not the sex itself, then the camaraderie that came with it, the giggling run to the bathroom after, with messy hair, to pee. I knew he was right, in theory, that we needed the tension to break between us every now and then, to help us feel like allies again, at least for a few hours. I wanted to feel the way I used to, that sex was where we best loved each other, that it was the why, the how.

I wanted to want to have sex. Does that count for anything? I knew that I'd enjoyed it once. The first few weeks Dustin and I were together, we had sex like I imagine any new couple does: right when we came in the door, again before bed, and then sometimes in the middle of the night, one of us waking up and reaching over and then, wordlessly, off we went. In the minutes before one of us was supposed to be out the door and on the way to work, we'd be tearing off the clothes we'd just put on and fucking on the edge of the bed. We'd met in September. He'd left the bookstore with me that night and I don't think we got a full night's sleep until we parted ways for Christmas.

Even before I met Dustin, I'd spent years pursuing sex, obsessing over it, thinking of intimacy as the main reason to be alive or the surest way to feel alive. I suspected it was the key to understanding everything about people, all our shame and desire and hurt and joy. Now "a healthy sex life" seemed like an aspiration I should have but felt no connection to. Sex struck me as not just repugnant but quaint—the province of naive people who had too much time on their hands. People who didn't have children.

We finally found a parking spot and climbed out of the car on a backstreet. Dustin strapped the baby into the carrier on his chest, mumbled something, then took off walking in the other direction. Okay, then. I trailed behind them for a few blocks, lagging in mild protest, then finally gave in and asked him where we were going.

"Huh?"

"Where are we *going?*"

"Oh. Here," he said to me as he headed toward the door of what I now saw, with no small amount of horror, was our local progressive sex-toy shop. I want to say I laughed at this, one of those *Isn't that rich?* laughs, but in fact I viscerally recoiled, then nodded, quietly accepting my fate. As much as I didn't want to go in, I didn't want to talk about why I didn't want to go in even more. I dragged my tired body down the sidewalk in the sun, squinting at the door, which was tastefully lined with white craft paper to prevent any innocent passersby from catching sight of people like us rifling through heaps of dildos.

I cursed Dustin in my head as we approached the door, but my stream of *Fuck you*s was replaced by the sound of angels singing when I made out a sign Scotch-taped to the window: NO MINORS ALLOWED. My deus ex machina. I spun around, victorious.

The baby was strapped to his father's chest, his little socked feet kicking in the air, his arms waving. At eight months, he was at what I liked to call *peak baby*, the image you hold in your head when you hear the word *baby*. A minor, indisputably.

"No minors allowed!" I shouted, trying not to grin.

"Oh, it's fine," Dustin said, barreling past me.

I stood there frozen on the sidewalk, choking on words like a cowardly cartoon character at the mouth of a cave. That is to say, the sensible one. "No way! Hey! Dustin! No. We can't go in there with him!"

Dustin just shook his head without looking at me and flung open the door, swaying his hips, holding the baby's feet and jostling him around in defiance. He was so clearly the mother I'd never be; everything came naturally. I followed, head low. What choice did I have?

The store was full of people even though it was the middle of the afternoon on a weekday. Everyone looked up—sex toy in hand—to gape at us when we came through the door. I shut down in that specific shopping way, the one where you walk in circles around the store, touching nothing and feeling hollow.

Dustin wagged vibrators under my nose like they were smelling salts, blue and pink and purple. They all seemed small and sad and snailish. I turned them all away. "What's wrong with it?" he said, holding something sleek and egg-shaped.

There was a time when I loved vibrators, maybe too much. When I was single, when I was virginal, when I was working from home all day. I ordered a waterproof vibrator, the Blue Dolphin, as an undergrad and would make a show of putting it into my shower caddie and walking down the hallway with it to the communal showers. I buzzed myself on random afternoons in the room I shared with two other women, hiding behind our three bureaus in case either of them came home unannounced.

But now I had the real thing, and that was problem enough. *Postpartum knife dick* is the term women in my Facebook-moms group coined to describe the shooting pain some of us got when we tried to do it. It was as if my body were sticking up for itself when my mind couldn't be trusted. The parenting websites warned about it, referencing *vaginal dryness* (someone should really come up with a better term for this) brought on by the drop in estrogen that comes when you give birth. They said that breastfeeding would prolong this state of being literally and figuratively sucked dry. I believed this information, found it comforting, even, but I also couldn't help but feel betrayed that my own body had succumbed to it. I was surprised to discover how much pride I had felt about something as involuntary as vaginal lubrication, that moment when a man is taken aback, whispering, "You're so wet," in the dark.

I wanted my body to do the talking for me. I wanted to carry around a printout explaining the hormonal makeup of a postpartum, breastfeeding woman. I wanted a valid excuse, a scientific one. *It's like menopause, hormonally.* I wanted a counternarrative to the finger-wagging keep-the-spark-alive message I'd internalized so deeply.

The parenting books, at least, were understanding. They said you were tired. That you were worried the baby might start crying as soon as you were, against all odds, about to come. They said you might be "adjusting to your new body" or actively denying the reality of it. You might be tensing up as you waited for him to touch your C-section scar and the surrounding area, which was, in a way that made you feel short of breath, still numb and might always be. You might feel "touched out," they said, as if a sentient sack of potatoes were always, somehow, right on top of you. You might feel, even when the baby was asleep in his crib, like some part of you could not, might never, fully relax again. To lose yourself in the way that good sex required felt dangerous or impossible when you were so inextricably entwined with someone else. Who was not your partner.

I also spent enough time reading baby forums and Facebook-mom groups to know that I wasn't alone. I knew other parents let sex disappear from their lives, telling themselves they were simply too busy or too tired. Some people claimed they didn't feel bad about it; they just figured they'd get around to fucking each other again eventually. Other women, under the cloak of anonymity, were more righteous: "I gave him a *child*. The least he can do is jerk it in the shower and not complain." I tried reading a post like this out loud to Dustin once, passive-aggressively, but it blew up in my face when he told me it would be "so hot" if I told him to go jerk off.

As much as I resented the pressure, I wasn't ready to embrace a sexless relationship. Part of me worried that if I gave up on summoning sexual desire now, at this seemingly critical juncture, it would never come back. What if my body forgot? What if I lost the thread entirely? What if I woke up a few years from now and I was a Diane Keaton character in a turtleneck, screaming because my husband saw me naked? It didn't seem that far off, honestly.

Another camp seemed to treat sex-after-kids as a sort of solemn duty. Women who took this approach believed sex to be a vital part of a romantic relationship and tended to be horrified by anyone who neglected it. All it took was a few minutes of obligation, of joyless effort, to keep him pleased, they argued. Wasn't this sort of sexual compromise worth it in the long run? I'm sure Dustin would have agreed. He used to claim that his worst nightmare was me letting him fuck me but secretly checking out in my head, unable to communicate that I didn't want to keep going. But that was before we had the baby.

Maybe the duty-sex women were onto something; maybe an obligatory hand job every couple of nights could have kept us connected. But something about that never sat quite right with me. Wasn't it hard enough, as a woman, to remember your own desire? I worried that if I took wanting it out of the equation, I'd slip into some default feminine mode and lose any ground I'd gained. I imagined myself faking orgasms, dissociating from my body, ignoring what I actually wanted for so long that I'd no longer be able to remember wanting to have sex for its own sake.

Either approach seemed like a betrayal of self at a time when I didn't have much self to spare. I said no to sex because it was something I could still say no to, because how

I felt was so new and complex, I needed to figure it out. I knew that if I didn't, I would start layering obfuscations over it until I couldn't go back. So I claimed my body for myself whenever I could. I guarded against all intruders, even if the intruder was the man I lived with, a man who loved me in all my complexity. I was all he wanted, he told me. And I just couldn't give myself to him.

I followed Dustin around the sex-toy store, doing a bad impression of someone being a good sport. A supportive partner. I let him hand me cartoonish dildos and held them and tried to look amused even though I wanted to throw them in his face. I felt like I was in the wrong room at a party, like I'd accidentally wandered into the host's bedroom. I was afraid to sound unreasonable. I was afraid I was being unreasonable. I didn't know yet that a willingness to share your unreasonable feelings was part of what love was. Communication and all that crap. We used to tell each other everything, back when everything was good.

"What's wrong?"

"Nothing."

I thought about how I should probably tell him that sometimes when he was looming over me in missionary position and I was staring up at the ceiling, flat on my back, enduring it, I got flashbacks to childbirth. To being immobile, fight-or-flight adrenaline rushing through my body but numb from the chest down, my abdomen sliced open.

I couldn't tell him because I wasn't sure I would ever really come back from it or from the feeling that these experiences were related, that they both felt, or made me feel, essentially female.

I knew that fucking was a shortcut to that allied feeling we were missing so acutely as we went about our zero-sum workdays, but even on the nights when I thought, *Okay, I would be open to sex,* I'd still rebuff him when he reached out to me, feeling like I didn't have the wherewithal to face down all the possible outcomes. Would I get the knife dick? If I managed to relax physically, would my fear of it still manage to ruin the moment because I was just waiting for the pain? Would I lie there trying to remember what it was like before, when I hated my body less (but, let's be real, still hated it), when at least my pussy was in working order, a source of pleasure, function, confidence. Would he notice I was in my head and then stop and ask me if I was okay, and would I then cry? If I cried, would I try to hide it, bury my head in his shoulder and hope he didn't notice? If he did notice, would he stop abruptly and lie next to me and ask what was wrong, and would I turn my back to him and stare at the wall, unable to explain?

I stood, listless, before a display rack of cock rings. "Hey," I said, pointing at them. "These are cheap." Dustin walked over to me holding a vibrator with Bluetooth capability in one hand.

"Oh, yeah," he said. "Do you want to get one?"

I shrugged. No, I didn't want to get one. But if we had to get something, I didn't want to spend more than $8.99. I looked up to see the baby reaching down with his chubby baby fingers to touch the tip of the vibrator Dustin was holding, and horror passed over my body in a wave. That was it. I snatched it (the vibrator) from him, lay it down on the display case, and, without saying a word, turned and fled, flinging open the paper-lined door and catching my breath outside in the cold air and sun. I took off down the block but had only a moment or two to myself before Dustin was beside me, irate, asking me what my problem was.

I kept walking away from him, shaking my head. This is a move I managed only on occasion but always found invigorating. A failure of maturity, even character, yes. A result of my inability to say how I feel, of stuffing it down and down until I couldn't keep it in anymore and off I went, moving purposefully, finally, and without looking back. I'd make it a block or two in whatever direction was away from Dustin and then, having broken free, I could feel my pulse slow.

When he caught up to me this time, I stood there frozen, trying not to laugh at the baby, who was happy as ever, not yet able to pick up on all the rage between us. I hoped.

"What's going on," Dustin said sharply, fed up.

"Sorry," I blurted. "But being in there...it's like you're rubbing it in my face."

"Rubbing what in your face?"

"Uh, the fact that I have no sex drive? That breastfeeding has dried me up, left me with nothing? That I don't even recognize my body anymore, and it's terrifying, and you have no idea what it's like? And instead of asking me how I am, you just bug me and pout about how you're not getting laid. How would you feel if you lost your sex drive?"

Dustin looked at me, confused.

"What?" I said, crying, trying to get out of the way of people walking by us on the sidewalk.

"I didn't know you didn't have a sex drive. You didn't tell me that." He was choked up, almost whispering. Stricken. I didn't know whether to laugh or cry or yell. *What?* I thought I was telling him every time I rolled away from him in bed, every time I flinched when he reached out to me, when he slipped his hand down my pants or up my shirt.

"It's a thing that happens to a lot of people, you know! It's totally normal, but no one tells you!" I was like a lawyer building her case.

"I didn't know!" he said. Both of us were incredulous.

"Well, then, what did you think was going on?" I said.

"I dunno, I just thought you didn't want *me*."

"What?" I said. I got a sinking feeling in my stomach, seeing the past nine months of our life tick by as if in a movie montage, moments where I thought he knew what I was thinking. Wouldn't he have noticed if he weren't so stuck in his own fuckless story? Shouldn't he have known? Apparently not.

"So you really didn't know?"

He shrugged, clearly hurt. "You never told me." Throughout this conversation, he was bouncing the baby.

I wanted to lie down right there, in front of the Japanese stationery shop, and never get up. Why had I never told him? When did life get so delicate, I wondered—both too tenuous and too cherished—for me to say certain things out loud? The stakes were higher, the thoughts were darker, and our relationship was weaker than it had ever been.

Didn't I used to say whatever was on my mind? *What's the worst thing that could happen?* I would ask myself. *We break up? We're sad? I have to find a new apartment?*

Now Dustin still felt familiar but not quite safe to confide in, like he was too invested in my feelings for me to be honest with him. When all your thoughts are shitty and even you don't trust them, why communicate them to the person you are supposed to love the most? Or so went the argument in my head. My feelings felt dangerous. Potentially destructive. I'd spent almost a year waiting for him to understand, to grant me a dispensation, to recognize that our dry spell was just one part of a bigger, scarier paradigm shift. I wanted him to see that I was scared, too, that we wanted the same thing, real intimacy. But first I wanted him to leave me alone. I didn't want to have to tell him.

Maybe I had been too ashamed to say anything. I tried to imagine a parallel universe, one that was kinder and more forgiving. One where I was kinder and more forgiving. Where a dry spell after kids was seen not as some moral failure, a reproductive bait-and-switch for men to groan and joke darkly about, as if we women had trapped our partners and now had no more use for them. A universe where I wasn't paralyzed, afraid to face what I had interpreted as "a bad sign," a failure (mine) of imagination or nerve. A failure to connect.

But I hadn't told him anything. I'd just turned my back to him in bed.

"Let's just go to the car," I said.

"Okay," he said, and we headed off into the sunset, defeated. We rode home not-talking to each other, which was easy to do with the baby there.

If only I could have seen into the future then, by some act of grace, and known for sure that things would be okay. I could have sat Dustin down and told him to wait for me on the other side. *Let's let the dust settle and accept that I'm a nursing mammal and everything's in flux and we're scared but know that in a year or so, everything will be different. One day the baby will nap for three hours every day and on the weekend, after we both go to our respective corners and stare at our phones long enough to regain a sense of equilibrium, one of us—okay, it'll still be you—you will creep down to whatever room I'm in and I'll be happy to see you. Know that I won't jump at your touch, that I won't turn my back to you, that eventually I will feel an almost adolescent reawakening of desire, that of course it's always you I wanted, and want, that logistics and baggage and pressure and getting too into my own head will always be part of the equation, but someday, thank Jesus, I'll be genuinely horny again.*

In a week or a month from this February 13, we'll find ourselves in bed in the middle of the day, and after another botched attempt at sex, I'll confess to him about the birth flashbacks I get sometimes when I'm on my back, pinned down. We'll cry together in bed and it'll be the beginning of the end of my avoiding him and avoiding difficult conversations. I'll know, soon, that just because something is hard and takes work and doesn't come naturally doesn't mean it isn't worthwhile. It doesn't mean anything. I'll know that as long as we can talk to each other, we aren't doomed. But we have to do it on purpose. We have to try now. Ugh.

The next morning, our first Valentine's Day as parents, I dragged myself out of bed as soon as I heard crying and carried the baby downstairs. I put boots and coats and hats on both of us and set him on the front porch—"Stay there, okay?"—while I struggled to unfold the stroller and carry it down the steps to the sidewalk. Soon we were off into the gray morning. Doughnuts. Coffee. That would have to do. When we got back, I fried Dustin an egg in the shape of a heart and wrote *We love you* in hot sauce around the edge of the plate. When Dustin came down the stairs a few minutes later, I looked at him and felt, if not love, then an echo of it. Enough to know it was still there somewhere and would eventually find its way back up to the surface.

Extra Room (1 to 26)

1.

WHEN THE BABY is still small and waking up at all hours of the night, we take a trip to Portland, Oregon. It rains every single day we're there and I spend most of the trip in the back of the rental car with our wailing baby, dangling my tit over his car seat. We meet people we know from the internet at food trucks and they swear the weather isn't always so bad. "I think, if I was able to enjoy things right now," I say to Dustin, "I'd really like it here."

We want milder weather, a real backyard, a change of scenery, a washer and dryer. I'm tired of carrying the stroller up the steps from the subway and waiting forever at restaurants. It's the typical story: the hard parts of living in New York have eclipsed the magic, and once you lose

sight of the magic, the whole project of living there becomes absurd.

I find a Craftsman house in Portland for rent on
Craigslist. We tell our friends, who are excited but also a
little betrayed. "It just seems so sudden," Halle says, but I remind her we've been talking about leaving for years. It's just
that now, time moves differently. I can see it passing. I can
see that we have to act.

We reserve one of those hellish pods that always seem bigger than they are, and I entertain the baby while Dustin and
his dad pack half our stuff into it. We leave the other half
on the street outside of our apartment. There's no time for
a farewell tour. We have a good-bye party at a bar on our
last Sunday afternoon, but I feel gone already. We leave New
York just before Christmas.

2.

Our new house has all these extra rooms. A finished basement. I use the washer and dryer almost every day, just
because I can. I've never been anything but a mom here, and
maybe because of that, I feel less self-conscious bringing the
baby to restaurants or pushing his stroller down eerily quiet
blocks. All the friends of friends we've been introduced to
here are married and own their houses. Everyone cooks. Has

a car. The trappings of adulthood are more conventional, more attainable here. We've attained them. In another life I might see this as a sort of bourgeois death but to me right now, it feels like coming up for air.

3.

One of my New York friends introduces me over e-mail to Danielle, who lives in Portland and has a baby a few months older than mine. "You can be mom friends. *No pressure.*" My impulse is to put her off, to reach out some afternoon when I'm feeling more myself. It's hard to see why anyone would want to be friends with me when none of my clothes fit and I am too tired to have a sense of humor.

On our first weekend in Portland, Danielle follows up with me and I invite her over. I buy a cake from a bakery down the street and remind myself to offer her tea. It feels like we are going on a date.

She knocks on our door and I swing it open to find her on the porch; she's wearing clogs, a drapey white sweater, and no makeup. She has long wavy blond hair and a baby slightly larger than mine on her hip. She comes in and takes off her shoes and the baby's coat and then sits down on the rug. We ask each other questions and move from nervousness to tentative ease. Our babies flop and crawl over the rug and each other like puppies while we eat cake. Neither of us is getting much sleep and we are both still breastfeeding around the clock. "It's so fucking hard," Danielle says, popping out a boob when her baby cries.

"Yes!" I say, and some part of me relaxes. Have I just been waiting for someone to come along and say it out loud?

"What was your birth like?" she asks me, and I narrow my eyes and shove a piece of cake in my mouth. "Fucking awful."

"Mine too," she says, and we laugh the kind of laugh that changes midway through into something darker. We make eye contact and nod, shake our heads, and then laugh more, full of resignation, laughing at the absurdity, saying more with a look than we had the energy to explain.

We take turns telling our birth stories and cuddling each other's babies and I feel myself getting manic with the thrill of finally being understood. The ability to be casually despondent, to complain to someone in shorthand and not feel like you have to insert disclaimers about how much you love your baby—I feel like if I could just be around her forever, I would be okay.

Danielle was also in labor for close to forty hours, she tells me. She also had the dream of the perfect birth, but she didn't give up and get the epidural like I did. Her baby, when he finally came, came barreling out of her so quickly and so traumatically, she got an extremely debilitating fourth-degree tear. She'd been seeing a pelvic-floor therapist, a godsend, and was healing and progressing, but sex was still something she couldn't quite contemplate. She couldn't ride her bike or go running. For the first few weeks, she couldn't even sit down. Despite all that, she went back to work when the baby was six weeks old. She didn't have a choice.

"It was really dark," she says.

"No kidding."

"I imagined all these things I'd do on my maternity leave."

"Ha."

"Exactly."

Talking to her, I realize that when I replay my own labor in my head, a sort of compulsive Monday-morning quarterbacking I can't stop doing, I imagine that if I had only "stuck it out" and had the vaginal birth I aspired to, everything would have gone perfectly. But there are all kinds of ways for things to go badly.

4.

We've been putting off looking into day care even though we both desperately need more time to work. Something about the task of Googling, scheduling tours, and filling out applications feels insurmountable. Maybe we just don't want to admit to ourselves what is becoming obvious: our little arrangement is not working.

"What if we just wait till he crawls?" I suggest. It seems as reasonable as anything else. Something about the fact that the baby would be mobile, able to move from one corner of the room to another at least, makes it easier to imagine abandoning him.

We need more money, which means we will spend $850 a month on day care and hope that, with the additional time to work, we will earn at least $851 more a month. The ridiculousness of this math is partly why we've spent so long splitting the time ourselves.

"Our baby will be a baby only once, and I don't want to miss out" was the sort of thing I said when I was pregnant, imagining days full of nothing but wonder. It was the sort of message that was ambient on Facebook and parenting blogs. *You'll never get this time back*. It's a threat. What was work compared to being face to face with a life unfolding before you? Now I am increasingly convinced that I do want to miss out, at least a little bit. "Your baby will only be a baby once" sounds less like a threat than a small mercy.

5.

"If I could spend ten good minutes with him every two hours, that'd be ideal," I say to Danielle over drinks one night. "You know, when they're really small. And you just...look at them. And there's nothing to do. And you know you're supposed to talk to them but it feels insane. And you just, like, boop them with toys on the nose, like they're dogs... *boop*." I feel a wave of longing when I say this stupid word: *boop*. It was part of my baby language, always would be. I remember his laughter, his stillness, staring back up at me, how his eyes would flash at me a certain way and I'd be convinced we were communicating on some deeper plane, beyond words, and I want to take back all my wild urges to be elsewhere. Wasn't this life at its most elemental? Wasn't this what I was working toward with writing?

If only I had the sort of spiritual stamina to stay in profundity longer, to not find it oppressive after ten minutes.

6.

"Taking care of a baby is sort of like driving down the high-way," an old co-worker's wife told me when I was pregnant as we sat at a picnic table in their upstate backyard. "It's incredibly boring but you can't look away."

I remember thinking, *Oh, but it won't be like that for me.*

7.

It was hard to see this time with our son for what it was: an investment in another person, the sacrifice at the start of a long, rewarding project. It was like a hazing ritual, with all the hardest parts at the beginning.

Did it have to be like that? Did you have to get remade? Did you have to hide in the bathroom on your phone, go for long walks and cry? Did you have to hate everybody, yourself most of all?

I didn't want to simply endure, I wanted to *enjoy the experience,* to come out the other side of the gauntlet stronger, wiser, and—defying reason—more beautiful. I saw my ability to be present as a test of my character or of my bona fides as a mother: Was I going to be happy, or was I going to flail? Was motherhood going to make everything in my life better, make *me* better, or was it going to ruin everything?

I operated as if there'd be a verdict. An easy answer. A story. I operated as if we were setting the tone for the rest of our lives.

It did not occur to me that we could simply muddle through. Learn as we go. Change things later. Forgive ourselves.

8.

We go on a few day-care tours with the baby in tow. It's hard to imagine leaving him anywhere and feeling okay about it, but the last place we visit is impossible to criticize. The day-care director opens the door and welcomes us into a baby paradise, filled with soft mats and mirrors and reassuring women cuddling children and reading them stories. A herd of babies crawls toward us, some of them waving, some saying, "Hiiiii," in tiny voices as we gingerly make our way across the big room.

Dustin and I look at each other and shrug. "That was easy," he says as we get back into the car and go home, both of us feeling like we checked off a box.

"What are you going to do on your first day with child care?" Danielle says over dinner that night, her voice giddy. "You should do something fun, just for yourselves. Go out to lunch somewhere nice. Go to the fancy new sauna!" On the way home from her house, I get a follow-up text from her: Have sex in the middle of the day, with the sun streaming in through the windows!

9.

On the baby's first morning in day care, I sit with him on the rug for a while, then move him off my lap and try to interest him in some toys so I can slip away. I hand the day-care director a bag of frozen breast milk. "I'll come back at one to nurse him," I say, and she is chipper, happy to accommodate me. When I finally move toward the door, the baby chases me, crawling full speed toward where I'm throwing on my jacket and rushing to step into my clogs. He's red-faced and screaming. He can't believe what's happening. I feel nauseated as I fight the urge to run over to him and pull him to me, inhale his smell, pull up my shirt and feed him standing up in the entryway. I can feel some part of me close off, out of necessity. "I'll be back!" I promise him, pleading with him as if he can understand, then I slip out the door. I chant, *I'm sorry, I'm sorry, I'm sorry,* in my head as I walk home.

Leaving him feels *wrong.* I can't believe the power of it, the power he has over me, how it overwhelms all rational thinking. When I get home I pace around, nervously tidy the living room. I don't go upstairs to find Dustin. I know if I see him, I'll cry. I unload the dishwasher and text Danielle, who tells me to drink a glass of wine, even though it's ten a.m. I look around. The house is empty. There is no baby in the next room, flinging toys around, no baby underfoot, banging on a pot with a spoon. I feel like I am getting away with something. Like the dream where you find a new room in your house.

Dustin comes downstairs and over to me. "How was it?" he asks.

"He screamed," I say and I watch Dustin's face fall. Something about how he's sad too is what makes me cry into his chest.

"It will get better. And we have to do this. You keep saying you need more time to work. Plus it's good for him," Dustin tries. "You know, to be around other kids, to socialize."

"I think that's just something people tell themselves," I say, laughing as I wipe tears away.

"Well, fine. Tell it to yourself!"

10.

I get to the day care at one o'clock that first day having achieved very little in the way of work and even less in the way of having sex with my husband. I peer around the front door, and I can see that my baby is in someone's lap with a pacifier in his mouth. His face is red and splotchy; he looks defeated. I hurry over to him, and when I grab him to me, he lays his head on my shoulder and whimpers.

"He wouldn't take the bottle," one of the caregivers tells me, wincing a little.

"Did he cry all day?" I ask, even though I'm afraid to know the answer.

"Not *all* day. Just on and off." I try not to cry myself. This was exactly what I dreaded. *This for writing? This for time alone, to work?* I nurse him and hand him off, then go back home for a few hours, more on principle than anything else.

On the way home, past daffodils and tulips and people walking their dogs, I give myself a pep talk: *You have to do this or you will go insane. It's for the well-being of the whole family. He will get used to it. You will get used to it. It will be hard and then it will be okay.*

Knowing what I am capable of, what I need in order to be a good parent, a good person—it occurs to me that I had to have a baby to figure all of this out. I had to get more than desperate; I had to get low down before I could learn to see and then say out loud what it was I needed. I had to move away from New York. Get a therapist. Meet Danielle.

How I wish it had come easier, sooner. I wish these two things had happened in the other order: me learning what I needed and *then* becoming someone's mother. But it's better than nothing. When I return home, I go right back into my little studio in the backyard, a renovated garage I've wordlessly claimed. I put a bulletin board up, light incense, hang pictures, and line up my books. Books by other women. Some of them mothers.

11.

What if having a hard time adjusting to motherhood wasn't some moral failure or a failure of imagination? What if we thought of the whole endeavor like we do work? Like how a career starts out with a lot of dues-paying, a lot of indignity, a lot of feeling unappreciated and complaining to your friends but then incrementally gets easier or more fulfilling. You get better at it. It becomes part of you. And you start to think, *Well, what else would I do all day?*

Of course, it's not the same at all. But you can understand why someone wouldn't want to have a job. And you can understand why someone would.

12.

Dustin goes to pick up the baby an hour or so later, and once they're home we sit on the couch together—a trio again. I feel an unfamiliar lightness. It's five p.m. and I don't feel like a husk of a human being. I'm not wallowing in misery and resentment or full of rage over the endless question of what to have for dinner. When I nurse the baby, I hug him to me, savoring the feeling of his body pressed into mine.

13.

I take myself to yoga—the regular, grown-up kind, which I haven't done in years. There are no babies, but there are actual men, which is always weird. Creeping into a new studio, not knowing where to sign in or when to take off my shoes, makes me want to turn back, but before I can, a woman spots me. Perhaps sensing my unease, she leads me into the room and gestures to where I can put down my mat. Feeling a hundred eyes on my lumpen body, I sit there doing and redoing my ponytail, trying not to make eye contact with anyone. The teacher comes by and introduces herself.

"Do you have any injuries I should know about?"

"Well, I just had a baby," I blurt out, despite it not being quite true anymore. I went through the same thing at the hair salon a week ago. "Oh, how old is your baby?" the stylist asked, and I debated lying to her. I wanted to say the baby was brand-new. I wanted her to understand that I was not quite myself yet. I wanted her to be impressed that I was sitting there, in the salon chair, wearing eyeliner. I want to be granted a special dispensation. I want to extend the grace period indefinitely. To be graded on a curve, have people think, *She's not doing too bad, considering.*

I want the yoga teacher to understand why my arms will shake in downward dog, why I will spend most of the class in child's pose, hiding my face. Why I might cry in pigeon pose, with my leg pulled up under me and my new stomach brushing against my calf. I want her to know that I used to be able to do everything, that I used to be in better shape. I want her to know this isn't me.

"He's nine months old now," I volunteer before she asks me, shaving off a few months the way you shave ten pounds off your weight on your driver's license. "I had a C-section, though. But I should be fine."

She nods, making deep eye contact, and puts her hand on my knee. "Just take it slow and make any adjustments you need. You know your body best."

Do I?

14.

Our unspoken deal is I do the dishes most nights while Dustin gives the baby a bath. This means I get to be left alone to listen to podcasts. Most of what I listen to are interviews with people whose careers I am jealous of, writers mainly, people who are in the world. People who still live in New York. I am still in the world, sure, and still writing. In fact, I am writing more and earning more money than I did pre-baby, but I still feel left behind. I am always thinking, too much, about what I could do if I had the kind of time some of my friends have. My friends without children. I harbor fantasies of ordering in sushi and staying up all night working as I did in the old days. And yet, I know I never got shit done then either. It is refreshing, I suppose, to have something outside of myself to blame.

Tonight I take a break from careerism to listen to a parenting podcast called *The Longest Shortest Time*. The host is interviewing Ina May Gaskin, "the mother of modern midwifery" who wrote the books responsible for all my romantic ideas about natural childbirth.

The host confronts Ina May, telling her that the books made her feel like a failure when her birth didn't go the way she'd envisioned. "I was under this impression," she says to Ina, "and maybe it was the wrong impression, that you believed that all women could have, if not a pain-free labor, then at least, like, a relaxed labor?"

"No," Ina May says. "No! Not everybody has a great time. Sometimes it's really rugged, it's really hard. You're not alone if you felt like you experienced a lot of pain and you felt like you failed." When I hear this I put down the bowl I am scrubbing and brace myself on the sink and sob. I'm a little horrified by how much her words affect me and how much I needed to be forgiven by this woman I've never met for what I think of as my poor performance.

Then Ina tries to explain. "What if we just told people that it always really, really, really hurts?" she asks, and then she answers herself: "Well, that wouldn't be very good, because you'd get everybody so frightened."

15.

What if, instead of worrying about scaring pregnant women, people told them the truth? What if pregnant women were treated like thinking adults? What if everyone worried less about giving women a bad impression of motherhood?

16.

We learn that it's better if Dustin does day-care drop-off in the morning—the baby is more even-keeled around him, more willing to separate from him, the person without breasts. I do pickup. Every afternoon the baby and I leave day care with a "report card," a little half-sheet of paper that says when he pooped and how long he slept. For reasons I'm not totally conscious of, I always shove it into my pocket when they hand it to me, like it's a love letter I should read in private. At the first red light I usually dig the paper out of my coat and spread it over the steering wheel.

The best part is always the fill-in-the-blank. *I had fun:* ____ [reading books, playing outside, going to the park, playing with blocks]. I can't help but hang on every word, as if this little report promises to restore whatever his absence has temporarily displaced in me. (Authority? Intimacy? Control?) By the time we're home and walking in the door, I'm his mother again.

I know there is more to his day than what is on the slip of paper, but I have the whole thing memorized anyway. I dole out the details of it to Dustin over the course of the evening, as if I am omniscient when it comes to the baby. Until so recently, it felt like I was.

17.

Today I was playing on the couch with the baby, who is less and less of one every day. He was giggling and flinging his body around in a way that kept making my breath catch. Half joking, I patted the couch cushion, like *Lie down,* and he immediately did it. He fell flat on his stomach and, laughing, looked up at me. I laughed too, in awe and a little heartbroken that he'd learned some new trick that I hadn't taught him.

When Dustin passed through the room I interrogated him: "Did you teach him to lie down?" I demonstrated the gesture. The baby did it again.

"I didn't teach him that!"

It is the smallest thing but it made undeniable what just a few months before had seemed impossible: Our son has a life outside of us. Separate from us. He is his own person. On some days, this serves as the giant relief I've been waiting for, and other days, other hours, I feel an unforeseen pang of sadness in my solar plexus.

One day he will grow up and move away from us and we will miss him constantly. I'm still mad when he wakes me up with his screaming each morning. I still need time and space away from him, to think and read and work and feel like a person, even though I know that one day I will long for nothing but to hold him again.

18.

"We just can't do it; we can't bear to hear him cry." That's what we've been saying to other parents for months when the subject of sleep training comes up. As if we're just really big softies. As if some parents are unmoved by their babies' crying.

I am to sleep downstairs in the guest room, per Dustin's orders. "Oh! Okay," I say, trying to mask my delight. I haven't had an uninterrupted night's sleep in almost a year, and part of me can't believe my good fortune. I feel like we are taking control of our lives. I also feel somber, oddly parental.

After taking a warm bath, I spend a few hours watching *Friends* with noise-canceling headphones on, trying to pretend the whole thing isn't happening. I think I hear crying a few times but it seems far off, someone else's baby. But when I get up to pee, there it is: Wailing. Sustained screaming. My nipples immediately harden and my milk comes in. I try pacing around the house, getting a drink of water, checking the locks on the door. I feel like a caged animal, unable to do her animal job. I sit up in bed staring at the wall, trying to be still but fighting the urge to rush upstairs and scoop up the baby. Eventually I can't stand it anymore, and I kick off the blankets and run upstairs to Dustin, who shoos me away without speaking.

"Let's just stop," I beg in a stage whisper.

"No!" he says. "Go back downstairs before he hears you." I can hear the baby, my baby, whimpering to himself.

"Let's just try it again in a few weeks. When he's older." I start crying. "I feel so bad. I don't want to do this." Hearing the baby cry and not comforting him feels like torture, like being starving with a meal in front of you that you're not allowed to eat.

"We're doing it," Dustin says with finality. He goes in to pat the baby on his butt and tell him everything will be okay. "We're right here." Are we? I crawl back downstairs and, blessedly, fall asleep. After two more nights of hell, it is done and everything is better and we are left wondering why we didn't do it sooner. The feeling that we have taken things into our own hands is intoxicating. What else can we do? What else haven't we done?

19.

I am not sure what to do with my newfound free time in the evenings. I hide out, paint my toenails, watch TV, think about how maybe there are just some people who are baby people and some people who aren't, and I'm not.

20.

I pick up a writer friend from her hotel downtown. Edan is here to give a reading. She published a bestselling novel last year and now it is out in paperback, and she is pregnant with her second child. While we're in the car on the way to lunch, I fiddle with Google Maps and ask about her flight, her new book, her pregnancy.

"I mostly can't wait to breastfeed again," she tells me.

"What?" I say.

"Oh, yeah," she says, "I loved it. That's basically why I'm having another kid."

"Wow," I say. "Huh." *Wait, did I like it too?*

With stuff this big, almost any way of looking at it can be true. We all talked like we were going to eventually reach some grand conclusion, some correct *stance,* but in fact it was different for everybody, impossible to pin down. Was childbirth traumatic or transcendent? Was pregnancy a time of wonder and awe or a kind of temporary disability? Were we supposed to fit our lives around our children or fit our children into our lives? My feelings changed every minute, depending on my mood and on the company I kept. It felt essential, though, to keep asking the questions.

21.

I want the hormones out of me. I want to be my old self again, as if that were possible, and I fantasize that once my boobs dry up, everything will be back to normal. The all-consuming project of early motherhood will be completed. I'll be out on parole.

I spend a week not really sitting down around the baby. Not holding him in my lap for too long. I disappear at bedtime and feel like I've forgotten something essential. Like I've left the house without locking the front door.

In a matter of weeks, breastfeeding becomes some far-away thing I did for a while. He seems to have forgotten it ever happened. It was once so important to me to make it to a year of breastfeeding, and now that I've done it, it feels like having really good SAT scores—no one cares once you get into college.

In any case, the baby has started to give more hugs and kiss me on the mouth. He says words. Something has shifted in me too. When he walks into the room, I slide onto the floor without thinking, reaching my arms out. I feel real joy at the sight of him, less fear. I laugh with him more easily. I dread leaving the house to go do work.

22.

When the baby is fourteen months old, Dustin's sister comes to visit. It is September, the two-year anniversary of our engagement. The idea of a wedding is still on the back burner but we decide to take advantage of having family in town to spend the night in a hotel.

I am nervous to spend the night with Dustin alone, uninterrupted. No excuses. But also giddy. On a friend's advice, we fuck as soon as we check in to the hotel room. I am laughing at myself in my head but it's fine; good, even. I feel we have overcome some mental trap, some pressure, as we glide into the hotel restaurant with tousled hair, easy smiles.

We spend too much money, buy a pack of cigarettes just because we can, get cocktails in a dark basement bar and then smoke under an awning, in the rain. The air is cool and we are a little drunk. I have never felt so free, so happy. It occurs to me I had a baby just to feel this free when I'm away from him.

23.

Wait, I text to Danielle after telling her how much better things have been lately, how great the baby is, how I feel like I'm experiencing real joy for the first time in as long as I can remember. I think maybe I have been depressed this whole time? Like, postpartum depression?

It never occurred to me that you didn't have PPD, she writes back. Danielle, my dearest godsend of a friend, who never knew me before I was a mother, never knew me not-depressed, and spent time with me anyway, for some reason.

I hate Dustin, I text her.

Why?

For not seeing it! I write. For not knowing!!! I think of all the times I felt like he was judging me for sleeping in, for snapping at him, for lying on the couch miserable instead of playing with the baby. It doesn't occur to me to be mad at myself. Or sad. Or to simply be grateful that whatever it was is now lifting. Has lifted. Danielle tells me not to make it about him, not to make it about the blame. That we've both been overwhelmed. He has his own shit; we should just keep moving forward. I don't quite agree with her. I'm not there yet, but I can see her point.

Just focus on the joy, she writes.

Ugh, fine.

24.

When the women at day care tell me that he gives his pacifiers to the younger babies when they cry and kisses them on the nose, I know what they're about to say.

"Yeah, he loves babies," I say, chuckling as I put on his winter boots.

"You should give him a baby brother or sister!" There it is. Everyone knows you're not supposed to say this sort of thing, but people can't help themselves. Part of me wants to give in and play along, to submit to the natural way of things, to loosen my newfound grip and go flying off the side of the cliff again. *Okay, fine, I'll have another baby. Because you want me to. Because it would be really cute.* To give up on the land of the living—the land of deadlines, of yoga classes, of happy hours—and dwell, again, in even more tenderness.

I just shake my head as I button up my son's fleece coat, then stand up with the baby on my hip and smile at them. "We'll see!" I always feel like such a mom at day-care pickup, waving good-bye to the women I pay to watch my kid so that I can write. These women who know nothing about me, have no idea how I feel about any of this. They want me to go back to the beginning. They want me to do it all again.

25.

How to explain the strange arc of parenthood to new mothers? How to tell it so that they believe you? The way things start out hard and then ease up. It is like finding more hours in the day. It is like the end of the school year, that first day of summer. It's like you moved to a new country, and it's beautiful but there's a war going on. But then the war ends and you begin reconstructing yourself.

My therapist calls it *expansiveness*. She makes a fist, then splays her fingers out into an open palm. You expand and retract. You are on defense, and then not. You are under siege and then not. You begin to open all on your own, to seek out other people. Seek out complexity of your own. You will lie on the couch during nap time and think about opening an old cookbook and making something complicated for dinner, just because. You will consider planting a vegetable garden this year. Or taking up running again. You will go to Target alone and leave with sunglasses, a new necklace. A set of cotton pajamas. Nothing for the baby at all.

26.

The baby and I walk home from day care together as the sun is setting. "Crow!" he says to each crow. *"Airpane!"* to each airplane. We stop every few blocks so I can look at him and kiss him in the crease where his nose meets his cheek. His dad, I know, is home making dinner, and will gasp and then yell from the kitchen, "You're home" as soon as we walk through the door. We will all stand there together in a hug. We are a family. Somehow it happened. Somehow I let it. Or else it happened despite me. In the end I find it doesn't matter.

Acknowledgments

I am so grateful for all of the women (and, okay, a few men) whose faith in this project kept me going as I stumbled through it.

For Sarah Smith, who met me when I still had a tiny baby at home and who assured me that I was onto something. I knew immediately that I could trust her to help bring whatever this was into the world. And for Jean Garnett's editorial genius, which has both saved me from and delivered me to myself time and again. These two women made it possible to write and publish this book without compromising vision or sanity, and I know how rare that is, and how lucky I am.

For everyone at Little, Brown, especially Lena Little, Jenny Shaffer, and Lauren Velasquez, who have been such good, smart company as we hustled this book into the world.

For Molly Fischer, Jen Gann, and Stella Bugbee at the Cut, who have made a space for complicated, intelligent writing about parenting (and everything else), and whose support made it possible to be a working writer.

Also for Mike Dang, who gave me my very first writing gig, and who later published my crazy birth story on Longreads. I wouldn't have trusted it anywhere else or with anyone else, and it led, quite directly, to this book.

For my writer friends, who read drafts, indulged my panic, inspired me with their own writing, and distracted me with good gossip. Thank God for brilliant women like Emily Gould, Charlotte Shane, Jessica Stanley, Anna Wiener, Lydia Kiesling, Edan Lepucki. And also Rumaan Alam, the rare man I allow into my DMs.

For my friend-friends, who make me feel so lucky. Halle, Lindsay, Miriam, Ashley, Will, and Jen have kept me myself and kept me laughing (while also, obviously, welcoming my crying). For Danielle, my first and dearest mom friend, who sat with me in the thick of it and poured me wine and listened to my dark thoughts and then celebrated with me when things got better. (What would I have done if we hadn't met?) And for Kathryn and Alexis, my Caymums who I miss and feel fated to have met.

For women like Rachel Fershleiser, Kathryn Ratcliffe-Lee, Christine Onorati, and Amanda Bullock, who have coached me through and advocated for my work and this book in ways I will always be grateful for.

For my therapist, Ann Marie, who I met just in time. This

book would be seriously lacking in a level of self-awareness if not for her guidance. Yikes.

For all the moms on Twitter for showing me the way, and for knowing the difference between needing advice and needing to make a bad joke from a place of desperation. Same goes for all the writers.

To my actual mom, for always knowing I was a writer, even when I forgot.

For the coffee shops in Brooklyn, Portland, and the Cayman Islands that I have haunted while avoiding my family to finish this book: Variety, Blue Stove, Caffe Vita, Random Order, Paperman's, Cafe-del-Sol, Grand Central Bakery, and Heart.

Speaking of family: to Dustin, for telling me early on I could write whatever I needed to, and that I didn't need permission. Perhaps you didn't know what you were getting into? Thank you for sticking with me while I figured all this shit out (the book and the life in the book), while I learned it all the hard way, like I do.

And to H, who made us a family, the kind I wasn't sure I knew how to be until you showed us, with your curiosity and wonder and stubborn, stubborn joy.

About the Author

Meaghan O'Connell's work has appeared in *New York* magazine, *The Awl,* and *Longreads,* where she is a contributor. Previously, she has been a columnist for *The Cut,* a co-editor of *The Billfold,* and an early employee at the tech start-ups Tumblr and Kickstarter. *And Now We Have Everything* is her first book. She lives with her family in Portland, Oregon.